The
Masquerade

The Masquerade

A POETIC DRAMA IN FOUR ACTS

MIKHAIL YURIEVICH LERMONTOV

Translated by Alfred Karpovich

iUniverse, Inc.
Bloomington

The Masquerade
A Poetic Drama in Four Acts

iUniverse books may be ordered through booksellers or by contacting:

iUniverse
1663 Liberty Drive
Bloomington, IN 47403
www.iuniverse.com
1-800-Authors (1-800-288-4677)

ISBN: 978-1-4759-7617-5 (sc)
ISBN: 978-1-4759-7624-3 (hc)
ISBN: 978-1-4759-7618-2 (ebk)

Library Congress Control Number: 2013903359

Printed in the United States of America

iUniverse rev. date: 05/24/2013

In memory of
Irakliy Andronnikov, the unique Lermontov scholar,
from the Translator

The target audiences:

1) The avid General English-speaking reader who cares to expand his/her cultural horizons;
2) The college students and scholars who major in Drama;
3) The university students and scholars who major in the Russian literature and language;
4) Theater repertory companies in their drive to rejuvenate the repertoire of foreign classics;
5) Theater spectators who enjoy Russian classical plays which are not infrequent on American stage;
6) Russian (local or foreign) repertory companies staging M. Lermontov in Russian, now having a possibility to use the English translation in subtitles or supertitles;
7) Russian American theaters performing in English.

Contents

M. Lermontov—Artist: K. Gorbunov, 1841
Watercolors

Introduction:
Lermontov, his Time, Life and Legacy

Mikhail Yurievich Lermontov, a poet, a writer, and a playwright, is not well known in the English-speaking world. Born in Moscow (1814), he was brought up by E. Arsenieva, his wealthy aristocratic grandmother. His parents died after a short-lived unsuccessful marriage. This tragedy impacted the growing boy. The feelings of loneliness and sadness never left him. His grandmother gave him an extensive education at home. They lived in a village she owned. She also owned the people who lived in it. Serfdom (slavery of peasants) reigned in Russia. It was legal to physically punish the serfs or to sell them. Mikhail witnessed brutality and later became a champion of freedom and a hater of the Czarist regime.

E. Arsenieva hired a Frenchman to teach her grandson French, a must in the culture of nobility. This French teacher was once a soldier in the Napoleonic War of 1812. His stories inspired the young man to write the poem "Borodino" about the defeat of Napoleon's troops by the Russians. This is how Lermontov's patriotic ideas originated.

At the age of 14, Lermontov attended boarding school for the sons of nobility. Later, he continued education at Moscow University where he studied languages, ethics, politics and literature. Then, he moved to St. Petersburg to perfect his new knowledge at a more prestigious university. This school rejected Lermontov's credits from Moscow. His friends had persuaded him to enter the Cadet School from which he graduated with the officer's rank of cornet. All this time he wrote his poetry and prose. His rebellious spirit in poetry irritated the Czar (Nicholas I) and his administration. They controlled Lermontov as an officer and as a poet. He was commissioned to the Caucasus (South of Russia) where the troops were routinely stationed. Lermontov participated in several military operations but he was never awarded any mark of distinction. His personal life was not successful. At 26, Mikhail was not married. His several love affairs with married and unmarried women were failures, which only added to his usual melancholy. Mikhail was no pleasure to socialize with. He always laughed at his fellow officers who spoke exclusively French and had problems with the Russian language. In 1841 Lermontov was killed by officer Martynov in a duel. The poet was twenty-six years old. Duels were illegal in Russia at that time, so Lermontov's dead body was left in the torrential rain in the south of Russia, at the foot of the Mount of Mashuk. His miserable grandmother came to bury him.

Lermontov's prolific literary work is unparalleled in the Russian literature. Irakliy Andronnikov, a Lermontov scholar of the Georgian ethnic descent, spent about sixty years of his life to study Lermontov's legacy. Lermontov was never monotonous in his writing styles. He was an early Romanticist in his small lyric poems, often an imitation of Byron's works (apart from French and Russian, the poet knew English and German). His major long poems "The Demon" and "Mtsyri" are purely romantic ones painted in dark grim colors. The Demon wishes to be good but with one kiss he takes away the life of a Georgian nun he loves. He spreads the evil inadvertently because the evil is in his cold blood, and then he suffers in his eternal solitude. So does Arbenin, Lermontov's protagonist in "The Masquerade". He is a villain who suffers together with his victims because the "demon" is in him. A thick layer of melancholy is deep in the poet's personality. A beautiful match for it is the scenic panorama of the Caucasian Mountains, turbulent rivers, rapids, and snow summits. Lermontov's nationalism never "malignifies" into chauvinism, despite his military background. On the contrary, he glorifies

Georgia, Chechnya, Dagestan and their proud, freedom-loving non-Slavic peoples, including Jews.

His idol was A. Pushkin, and Lermontov is placed second to Pushkin. "The Masquerade" was revised by Lermontov three times to please his censors and content editors. When Pushkin was killed in a duel (1837), Lermontov wrote a poem "The Poet's Death" in which he accused the political system of Pushkin's death. His attacks on the regime did not remain unnoticed. The Czar and the elite tried to ostracize the poet.

By 1832 Lermontov had already written 200 lyric poems, 10 long poems, and three plays. Only "The Masquerade" was a poetic drama. The other plays were written in prose. "The Masquerade" appeared in 1835. In the poet's life time, it was not staged. It was first staged in 1852. The poet was advised to change the content and the intrigue in order to ease up the tension. "The Masquerade" expresses the Zeitgeist of the Russian Romantic period in its transition to critical realism. One hundred years later (1941) the film version of "The Masquerade" appeared in Russia. It was a huge success. In today's Russia "The Masquerade" is staged rarely. Arbenin's monologs are passionate and pathetic. As to the dialogues, they are easy to read and true to life.

This Russian writer will be best remembered for his novel "A Hero of Our Time" (1840). The "hero" is Pechorin who, like the Demon or Arbenin, spreads the evil carelessly, out of boredom, compromising his innate decency. Lermontov sides with the victims: strong men and fragile women of the Caucasus. The term "Caucasian" in its American sense is absolutely foreign to the Russian ear.

Many of Lermontov's small early lyric poems were later musically translated into the genre of romance. "The Demon" became an opera composed by A. Rubinstein. A melancholic waltz was composed by A. Khachaturian only for "The Masquerade". Lermontov's translations of Goethe and Heine from German, without any exaggeration, surpassed the originals. All of his works have been translated into English. Now Lermontov belongs to the world culture.

As his admirer I am still in mourning. If Lermontov had lived longer, he could have created more masterpieces. His mission was not entirely accomplished.

A Note from the Translator

This is the first ever poetic translation of M. Lermontov's "Masquerade". The translator attempts to meet the following challenges:

(a) The routine, but not trivial, techniques of rhymes and rhythms: where hunting for melodious rhymes fails or distorts the meaning, the translator succumbs to a relative "safety" of BLANK VERSE. M. Lermontov himself, though sporadically, employs BLANK VERSE, following A. Pushkin's tradition.

(b) The translator has chosen some kind of "common denominator" within a long chain of the English language historic development, at least, between Shakespearean Early Modern English and Modern English. This cautious approach allows to imitate the Russian flavor of the 19th century Golden-Age poetry. On this path certain ups and downs are imminent. The characters' speech varies with situational changes quite widely, from plain Russian (in this case, plain English) of gamblers to highly emotional or meditational monologues of the protagonists. Contemporary Americanisms are avoided. Nor are pure Briticisms favored. Certain archaic verb forms or French terms are not frowned upon. They contribute to the distinctive "aroma" of the 19th century Russian aristocratic culture. The translator has no better guidance in this work than his own linguistic taste supported or, at least, disapproved by several comprehensive English and Russian dictionaries.

(c) The translator remains faithful to the original text: Arbenin's romantic monologues do not present easy reading. The translator believes that some of the readers who know or learn Russian will be pleased to see how the original text disciplines the fine art of translation. Any translator is not a poet of his own right. This is not an authorized translation. Nor is it a literal one. It is, to the best of the translator's ability, supposed to be an artistic translation.

(d) The translator uses several 19th century water color reproductions taken from open sources: the poet's portraits (K. Gorbunov) and the "Masquerade" characters (N. Kouzmin).

Cast of Characters

Arbenin, Yevgheniy Aleksandrovich (pronounced "Ar-ben'-nin")

Nina, his wife

Prince Zvezdich[1]

Sprich (pronounced "Shprikh")

Baroness Strahl (pronounced "Shtrahl")

Kazarin (pronounced "Kazah'-rin")

Lady (Mask), same as Baroness Strahl

Gentleman (Mask), same as Stranger

An Official

Card Players: 1st player, 2nd player, 3rd player, 4th player, 5th player

Bank keeper (Dealer)

Guests

---

[1] It is a tradition in all translations from Russian to use the word "Prince" for "Knyaz" (Russian) as a title of nobility, not necessarily of royalty.

Petrov

Dancing ladies and gentlemen

Man-servants and Maids (Ivan and others)

Host, hostess

Niece, Lady, Doctor, Old Man

ACT 1

The officers are gambling in the playing house (N. Kouzmin)

SCENE 1

SUBSCENE 1[2]

(Players in the playing-house[3]. Prince Zvezdich, Kazarin, and Sprich.
Some punters are punting[4] and keeping the bank.
Others are standing around.)

First Player: Ivan Ilyich,
                  Please, let me place a bet.

Dealer: As you will, Sir.

First Player: One hundred roubles.

Banker: It's all right.

Second Player: Good luck to you.

Third Player: It looks so bad. You'll need good luck to get it back.

Fourth Player: Here goes!

Third Player: Let me place a bet!

Second Player: All in? That'll sting you!

---

[2]   Subscene 1 simplifies where possible, the card players' slang in
      this translation. Besides, following the original text, the translator
      sporadically uses Blank Verse in Scene 1.
[3]   gambling (playing) house. "Casino" was not used.
[4]   punt-punter: place a bet on a randomly chosen card (British)

Fourth Player: Listen, my friend,
                 Unless you shoot it high,
                 You won't get your pie.

Third Player *(whispering to the first one)*: Keep your eyes open.

Zvezdich: The whole thing works!

Second player: Hey, Prince, please keep your wrath restrained,
                 Don't let it spoil your blood.

Zvezdich: Keep your advice refrained,
                 At least, for now.

Dealer: It's covered.

Zvezdich: Damn it.

Dealer: Please, kindly pay.

Second Player *(mockingly)*: I see that you, in fervor, may
                 Gamble everything away.
                 What should I pay
                 For these epaulettes?

Zvezdich: They are with honor gotten:
                 My epaulettes are not for bail or sale.

Second Player *(grinding his teeth and leaving)*:
                 You'd better be more prudent
                 With your bad luck and at your age.

*(Zvezdich, after a glass of lemonade, is sitting down on
the side and is now engrossed in thoughts)*

Sprich *(with a show of sympathy):*
>   With money, Prince, I'll help you right away,
>   And in a hundred years you may
>   Return the silly interest.

> *(Zvezdich bows down coldly and turns away.
> Sprich takes leave dissatisfied)*

Subscene 2

*(Arbenin and others; Arbenin enters, bows, approaches the table;
then he beckons to Kazarin and steps aside with him.)*

Arbenin: Why aren't you playing, my Kazarin?

Kazarin: I look around, my friend, and see
            You've become a real "barin"[5],
            Married and rich, my dear,
            You quite forgot your chums and players here.

Arbenin: Oh, yes! It has been a long time.

Kazarin: What keeps you busy all the time?

Arbenin: Love is the name of business.

Kazarin: Taking your wife out to balls?

Arbenin: No.

Kazarin: Gambling?

---

5   "Barin": a rich and famous gentleman in tsarist Russia (Russian word)
     pronounced "bahrin". Also: master.

Arbenin: Not really . . . I sneak!

                I see new faces here. Who's that sport?

Kazarin: Sprich!
                You'll meet him right away.
                Adam Petrovich!
                (Sprich comes up and bows)
                Here's a friend of mine, Arbenin.

Sprich: I know you.

Arbenin: I don't recall, Sir, meeting you before.

Sprich: I've heard of you so much heretofore,
                By rumors, so that it became my dream
                To meet you once in person.

Arbenin: I regret,
                Of you I know not a thing,
                But you yourself will tell me everything.
                (Both bow to each other again.
                Sprich makes a wry face)
                I cannot really like him.
                I've seen a lot of ugly mugs,
                But that one
                Wasn't made for fun.
                What spooks
                Is his inhuman looks!
                Not quite the devil either . . .
                The tiny bugles of his eyes
                As well as his malicious smiles . . .
                What may his ugly face present
                I wouldn't be able to invent!

Kazarin: My friend,
He may
Look devilish, indeed,
But he appears
A good friend in need.
The minute you address him
The money's there;
To decent people
He is most fair;
With "Jesuits" he's a "saint",
A wicked gambler, he won't faint.
Not once has he been beaten!
With atheists he'd even dare
Godless to be; his whole life is care
To know all and to remember everything.
As to his background, I know not a thing.
Most likely, he's of the Jewish stocks
As there're so many tongues he talks.
In short, you're going to like him, I'm sure.

Arbenin: The portrait's good. It is the model that I can't endure.
Look at the man: he's powdered, mustached, and tall;
Must hang around some fancy hall,
An expert shot, but not a hero in a battle,
A rake in resignation,
In foreign lands
He found his probation?

Kazarin: You're almost right.
His regiment expelled him for a duel
Or because he didn't want to fight,
He had a feeling
He must refrain from killing.
His mother, too, was very tough,
And then again, after five years,
He took another challenge:
This time the fight was very rough.

Arbenin: That short one over there,
What is he like?
With his unruly tousled hair,
With his sincere smile,
A snuff-box and a crucifix?

Kazarin: Oh, Trushchov!
This priceless little jewel
Spent seven years in Georgia's warfare
Or was commissioned with some general there,
Behind a corner did he someone whack.
Five years he sat under the care
And got a CROSS around his neck.

Arbenin: You seem to know these new folks very well.

Players *(yelling)*: Kazarin, Afanasiy Pavlovich, come here!

Kazarin: I'm already near,
(with pretended interest)
Oh, hell! This treachery's not fair!
Ha-ha-ha-ha!

First player: Please, hurry up!

Kazarin: What's happening out there?
(A lively talk springs up among the players, and then they calm down. Arbenin takes notice of Prince Zvezdich and comes up to him)

Arbenin: Why are you here, Prince?
Isn't that the first time you came?

Zvezdich *(with displeasure)*:
        I've meant to ask you, Sir, the same.

Arbenin: Your answer is forestalled, my Prince,
I have been long around, and even since
Oft have I seen many a youth,
Hopeful and loving, who in the school of life,
Knew nothing of the truth . . . In their silly happiness.
I used to watch with awe
The wheel of fortune spin;
One was to win,
The other to be crushed.
Neither I envied, nor
Did I participate it in.
In their flaming souls
Their sole aim was love . . .
Death swiftly took the toll
In front of me, and seeing it again
Is going to be tough.

Zvezdich *(takes Arbenin's hand emotionally)*:
I have lost.

Arbenin: I see. So what? To drown yourself?

Zvezdich: Oh, I am in despair . . .

Arbenin: Two remedies are fair:
To give yourself a pledge to never gamble
Or at once to sit down and handle
The art to win,
Then you'll have to spin
And sacrifice them all:
Your friends, your relatives, your honor . . .
You'll have to touch and to experience,
Without passion,
The soul and faculties of their owner,
To tear them apart; without digression
To study well the strangers' faces,

Their intentions and even their thoughts,
For years to practice aces and more aces,
To think all day, to play all night,
To give yourself no relief in fight
And not to let them understand your plight . . .
To learn how to scorn the law of man,
The law of nature,
And not to tremble when
Someone around you, can
As "skillful" as yourself,
Besmear you a "rotter",
And to await the shameful end of luck
At any moment . . .

(Silence. The Prince barely listened and was excited)

Zvezdich: I know not what I shall do . . .

Arbenin: Whatever you would want.

Zvezdich: Perhaps, some happiness?

Arbenin: Oh, there's no happiness here.

Zvezdich: I did lose everything. Please give me some advice

Arbenin: For more advice I'm not wise.

Zvezdich: Well, I'll try again . . .

Arbenin: Wait, I shall sit instead of you.
              Like you, young as you are,
              I, too, was young and inexperienced once,
              Like you, presumptuous and foolhardy,
              And if *(Arbenin pauses)* . . . Some kind of buddy
              Had stopped me, then . . .

(Arbenin stares at Zvezdich and changes his tone)
Please ask your fortune to be fair,
The rest is none of your affair!
(Arbenin comes up to the table. He is given a seat)
Please don't say no to the "disabled" man,
I want to see what fate may have in store.
Will it betray its old fan
To the young offspring in your war?

Kazarin: He can't restrain himself, he burns with ardor.
              (softly) Hey, chum, you'd rather
              Not let them spatter you with mud,
              But show an old-timer's heavy thud.

Players: Well, you know best,
              You're the host;
              We're your guests.

First Player *(whispering to the second player)*:
              Now be all eyes
              And stay, please, on alert!
              This "Vanka Cain"[6] may hurt.
              With me he goes against the grain,
              Might even top my ace
              And bring me pain.

*(They begin the game, crowding around the table.
Sometimes screams are heard. As if to continue the conversation,
many leave the table and look grim).*

(Sprich leads Kazarin to the proscenium)

---

6   "Vanka Cain": 'Vanka', a form of 'Ivan' (Russian male first name), plus
     'Cain' (a biblical negative character). The figure of speech: looking
     innocent but, actually, dangerous.

Sprich *(mischievously)*: They have crowded into a lump,
               It seems a thundercloud is here.

Kazarin: He'll cow them for a month!

Sprich: It appears he's a good hand at it.

Kazarin: He was.

Sprich: He was? And now . . . ?

Kazarin: Now? Married, rich and gracious . . .
               "A little lamb" looks meek and mild,
               And yet, this beast is still audacious,
                    The beast is wild.
               To triumph over human nature,
                    To break oneself
               A silly thing to say.
                    Arbenin even may
               Assume an angel's looks,
               The devil in his heart still spooks.
               And you, my friend,
               (slapping him on the shoulder)
               A runt against himself,
               Bear a little devil in yourself.

(Two players come up talking in a lively manner)

First Player: Didn't I tell you?

Second Player: It can't be helped, my pal,
               It seems I've met my match.
               Didn't I cheat? But no, he beat them all, like hell!
               Shame is my only catch . . .

Kazarin *(coming up)*: Is he beyond your power, gentlemen?

First Player: Arbenin is the master.

Kazarin: Come on, my gentlemen.

(A ripple of excitement among the players at the table)

Third Player: Well, if he goes on like that,
    A hundred thousand he may bet.

Fourth Player *(to the side)*: He'll cut his throat yet.

Fifth Player: We'll wait and see.

Arbenin *(rising)*: Basta[7].

(He picks up the gold and leaves, with the others remaining around the table. Kazarin and Sprich are also at the table. Arbenin is pale. He takes the Prince by the hand and gives him the money.)

Zvezdich: Ah, I shall not forget,
    You've saved my life . . .

Arbenin: Not only: also your money you may get.
    (Bitterly)
    Indeed, it's hard to say which is a fairer strife:
    For money or for life?

Zvezdich: You've sacrificed for me a lot!

Arbenin: Not in the least. I felt perturbed,
    And I was glad at the anxiety
    That filled again my breast and mind.
    And where I sat to play,
    A battlefield you'd find.

---

[7]   Basta (Spanish and Italian): enough; still used in Russian.

Zvezdich: You may have lost the game.

Arbenin: Oh, no! Those blissful days are no more the same.
               I see them through . . . all their subtleties are fine,
               And therefore the game is no longer mine.

Zvezdich: My thankfulness eludes you.

Arbenin: To tell the truth, I do not bear
               Your thankfulness, I find it fair
               To set my foot
               Only for someone who is good.
               I've never had a binding obligation
               Unless I saw a profit from utilization.

Zvezdich: I don't believe you.

Arbenin: Who tells you to believe?
               Since ages weave,
               I've been used to it;
               If not my indolence, I would dissemble . . .
               Why don't we drop this talk to disassemble?
               (after a pause)
               It wouldn't be bad for you and me
               To have a little diversion
               On these holidays. At Engelhardt's[8]
               They, surely, have a masquerade . . .

Zvezdich: Yes.

Arbenin: Will you go?

Zvezdich: I won't say no.

---

[8]   Engelhardt: The owner of the building with its entertainments and
      restaurants for the Russian nobility of St. Petersburg.

Arbenin *(to the side)*: I will relax a little in the crowd.

Zvezdich: Some women must be paragons of beauty there,
            And they say some of them are . . .

Arbenin: Let them say that. Why should we care?
            All ranks are equal, covered with a mask;
            A mask has no title, no soul;
            It has a body, sole and whole.
            If facial features are disguised, it is the task
                The feelings to unmask
                And to be bold.

            (Both take leave)

SUBSCENE *3*

(The same characters, except for Arbenin and Prince Zvezdich.)

First Player: He came out in time and brought the trouble then.

Second Player: He should've saved a chance to remain sane.

Man-Servant *(entering)*: Dinner is served.

Host: Let's go, gentlemen.
        As you have lost,
        Seek consolation in champagne.

        (Everybody takes leave)

Sprich *(alone)*: It is Arbenin I would want to get much closer to,
And I do like to eat here for nothing.
(Putting a finger up to his forehead)
When I have dined, I'll find out something
And to the ball I'll fly with these two.
(Leaving and still mulling things to himself)

Prince Zvezdich is flirting with the Baroness (N. Kouzmin)

SCENE 2
Masquerade

SUBSCENE 1

(Masked people, Arbenin and later Prince Zvezdich.)
(The crowd shifts about on the stage. There is a settee on the left.)

Arbenin *(entering)*: Why am I seeking
Entertainment
In the crowd?
It's dazzling and it's buzzing all around . . .
My heart stays cold, and dormant is my fancy range:
They all are alien to me, to all of them I'm strange!

(Zvezdich approaches yawning)

Here's the generation of today.
When I was young, was I like him,
    If I may say?
Well, Prince, haven't you encountered an affair?

Zvezdich: I've been walking for an hour . . . Is that fair?

Arbenin: Oh, would you wish your luck to find you?
A novelty is here cooking,
You have to go out looking.

Zvezdich: All masks are silly . . .

Arbenin:	Oh, no! There's no silly mask;
	When they are silent, they are full of mystery,
	When they begin to chat, they're cute.
	One can impart to their words
	A smile, a glance, whichever really one wants!
	Look, for example, over there:
	A Turkish lady's nobly stepping, stout and fair,
	Look how tall,
	And how her breasts with passion swell,
	A proud countess or a princess? You can't tell.
	She could be a Diana in Beau Monde,
	A Venus in disguise,
	Or, possibly,
	This beauty finds it wise
	To visit you tomorrow night for half an hour . . .
	In either case you do not lose: you'll enjoy her power.
	(Arbenin leaves)

SUBSCENE 2

(Zvezdich and a masked lady)

(A domino approaches him and stops.
Prince Zvezdich stands engrossed in thought.)

Zvezdich:	Yes, this is all true, easy to tell . . .
	And yet, I'm still yawning,
	Here's one of them . . . God bless me!

(A masked lady separates herself from the others
and taps him on the shoulder)

| Lady: | I know you. |

| Zvezdich: | And intimately, it would seem. |

Lady: What you were thinking of, I know, I would deem.

Zvezdich: In this event, you're happier than me.
                 (he peeps under her mask)
                 But if I'm not wrong,
                 God gave a pretty little mouth to thee.

Lady: You like me? So much the worse.

Zvezdich: For whom?

Lady: For one of us.

Zvezdich: I don't see why, and I'm not condemned to doom,
                 And your prediction
                     Is a fiction.
                 Although I'm not quick-witted,
                 I'll discover who you are.

Lady: Then you may know how we converse it
                 And how far . . .?

Zvezdich: We'll talk and go our separate ways.

Lady: Right?

Zvezdich: You'll go left, and I'll go right . . .

Lady: But what if it's my purpose here
                 To speak to you and to be near,
                 What if I say that in an hour
                     You will swear
                 That to forget me is beyond your power,
                 That you'll find it fair
                 To sacrifice your life and die,
                     When I,

A nameless spirit, fly away,
And you would want to hear me say
One only word "Good-bye"?

Zvezdich: Since you're so smart, why do you waste your words?
             If you know me, say
             How I differ
             From all other nerds.

Lady: You're immoral, vain and spineless.
             You're but weak, wicked and godless.
             You're the mirror of this age,
             The modern glittering worthless page.
             You'd want to have a whole life in your possession,
             But all the time you steer clear of a passion.
             Possession—yes! Sacrifice—no!
             You wonder if I know you? Oh, yes, I do, I know . . .
             You, Sir, may want to own all,
             But cannot sacrifice at all!
             You treat the heartless, prideless
             People with some scorn,
             And yet, you ARE those people's pawn.

Zvezdich: I'm very flattered.

Lady: You did a lot of evil.

Zvezdich: Involuntarily, maybe.

Lady: Who knows? With you a woman should not be.
             Of that I'm aware.

Zvezdich: To look for love I do not dare.

Lady: To seek it you have no method.

Zvezdich: Tired of seeking, I should say.

Lady: What if one day
              She shows up to say
              "You're mine!" To remain heartless would you dare?

Zvezdich: But who is she? Of course, she's some angel.

Lady: No, just a woman. The rest is none of your affair.

Zvezdich: Please show her: to see her would be fair.

Lady: You wish too much. Think over what you said.
              (she pauses a moment)
              She wouldn't beseech your sighs or your confessions,
              Nor would she beg your tears, speeches and requests
                      Or fiery passions.
              You only have to take an oath to spare your effort
              To find out who she is and to be always silent.

Zvezdich: I swear on my word of honor, by heaven and by earth.

Lady: Well, let's go now, and mind it that between us
                      There is no mirth.

              (They go out arm-in-arm)

Subscene 3

(Arbenin and two masked individuals)

(Arbenin pulls a masked gentleman by the hand)

Arbenin: You, Sir, have cursed me, like a peasant;
              Things I've heard from you are so unpleasant

That a man of honor can't endure . . .
Do you know who I am?

Gentleman: I know who you were.

Arbenin: Take off your mask, and right away!
It's a dishonorable way.

Gentleman: Why should I, if my face is not familiar to you,
Just like my mask. Your own face to me is new.

Arbenin: I don't believe you. Somehow you show fear.
It would be shameful to be mad at you.
You're a coward, please do not come near.

Gentleman: Fare you well, my friend, but please be on your guard:
Tonight's misfortune is going to hit hard.
(He disappears in the crowd)

Arbenin: Wait! He's gone . . . But who is he?
This man has really gotten me worried.
Oh, no!
He was some cowardly foe?
To count them all there is no way.
Ha-ha-ha-ha! Farewell, my friend!
Have a good day!

SUBSCENE 4

*(Sprich and Arbenin. Sprich appears. Two masked ladies sit on the sofa.
Somebody comes up and intrigues them. He takes one of them by the
hand. She tears herself away, drops her bracelet and leaves.)*

Sprich: Yevgheniy Alexandrovich,
Whom were you pulling along there

And so mercilessly?

Arbenin: Oh, it was nothing.
              With a friend
              Just joking aimlessly.

Sprich: Were you? It was no laughing matter.
              As he walked, he scolded you relentlessly.

Arbenin: With whom?

Sprich: With someone in disguise.

Arbenin: You have big ears.

Sprich: I don't poke my nose with advice.
              I hear everything and remain silent . . .

Arbenin: I have observed that.
              It's so shameful and bad,
              You may not know that . . .

Sprich: What is it, Sir?

Arbenin: Forget it. I'm joking again . . .

Sprich: Please, tell me.

Arbenin: Your wife is beautiful, I hear?

Sprich: Well, so what?

Arbenin *(changing his tone)*: Is the man who's near,
              Dark and with moustache,
              Homing in on you?
              (He whistles some tune and leaves)

Sprich *(alone)*: You, dried-up throat, making fun of me,
                    Will make a cuckold of yourself
                    And get my full revanche[9].
                    (He gets lost in the crowd)

Subscene 5

(The masked lady, all by herself.
Excited, she enters quickly and drops herself on the couch.)

Lady: Oh, I'm out of breath . . . he chased me,
                   What if he'd snatched my mask and faced me?
                   He did not recognize me, and how on earth
                   He could suspect a woman, who is worth
                   The world of envy, would forget herself in passion
                   And would beseech him on his neck for only
                       Two sweet moments . . .
                   Without begging love, but begging pity,
                   Would boldly say "I'm yours" in her insanity!
                   For him this mystery is never to be solved,
                   And I shall never help him to unfold . . .
                       Yet, he does not want to leave without
                   Some souvenir . . . Well, my ring?
                       The risk is indescribable!
                   (She sees a bracelet and picks it up from the floor)
                   What a stroke of luck! Good gracious!
                   An enameled gold bracelet—so likeable!
                   Fine! With it, let him find me.

---

9   revanche (French): revenge. The Russian noblemen used some French
     in their 19-th century Russian Language, "Revanche" is still available
     in Russian..

SUBSCENE 6

(The masked lady and Prince Zvezdich.
Zvezdich elbows his way, holding a lorgnette.)

Zvezdich: Exactly . . . this is she
In the midst of thousands
    I will know her
(He sits down on the couch and takes her by the hand)
Oh, you won't run away.

Lady: I do not, Sir.
What do you want?

Zvezdich: To see you.

Lady: That's funny! I'm with you.

Zvezdich: This is an evil joke!
Your purpose is to joke,
My purpose is another . . .
I would rather
Rip off by force
That mask of yours.
The false countenance you wear
I would right now have to tear,
Unless this heavenly creature may
Open her features right away.

Lady: Oh, there is no way
To understand a man.
You're discontented. Is it not enough for you
    To hear that I love you?
    No, you would want it all!
You'd want to meet me at a fancy ball
Or at some party and with laughter to relate

A ludicrous affair.
You think it would be fair
With your friends my name to desecrate?
And help them to resolve their doubt
By pointing with your finger
You would, then, have to linger,
"This is she—the woman I can't live without".

Zvezdich: I will recall your voice.

Lady: Oh, come on! Try to approach women!
             Lots of us produce the same noise.
             Don't ever try to work a miracle!
             You'll reach the pinnacle
                 Of shame
             As women's voice is all the same.
                 And that would not be bad . . .

Zvezdich: My happiness is somewhat sad.

Lady: Well, who knows what?
             Why don't you bless your lot
             That I'm keeping this mask on?
             I could be old and ugly . . . what a pawn
             You could have made of me . . .

Zvezdich: You won't scare me away,
             And don't you think, I may
             Guess about the other charms of yours
                 By knowing half of them?

Lady: Fare you well for good!
             (She wants to go)

Zvezdich: Oh, one more moment, please! It would be good
              To give me something for a keepsake.
              Why don't you pity me?

Lady *(after two steps away)*: You're right. I pity thee . . .
              Pick up my bracelet for your sake!
              *(She throws the bracelet onto the floor. While he is
              picking it up, she disappears in the crowd.)*

SUBSCENE 7

(Zvezdich and later—Arbenin)

Zvezdich *(looking out for the lady in vain)*: She has fooled me. I have
              a reason
                    To go insane . . .
              (at seeing Arbenin): Oh!

Arbenin *(walking deep in thought)*: This evil prophet caused me pain.
              And scarcely was it a joke
              That he was trying to evoke.
              This man must know me . . .

Zvezdich *(approaching)*: Your recent lessons served me well.

Arbenin: I'm wholeheartedly delighted.

Zvezdich: And you can never tell,
              When lucky stars may fall on you.

Arbenin: Indeed, your luck is always new.

Zvezdich: No sooner had I caught her thinking "That is done",
              Than suddenly . . .
              (He blows on the palm of his hand)

Unless I dreamed this fun,
I've made a moron of myself,
   And now
To myself I boldly make a vow.

Arbenin: I know nothing how you conflict,
              And therefore I do not contradict.

Zvezdich: You're still joking, but a friend, indeed,
              Is someone who is a friend in need.
              I'll tell you everything.
              (Whispering a few words in Arbenin's ear)
              I was so daunted!
              The charmer got away,
              And here's *(he shows the bracelet)*,
              Like I were haunted
              In a dream.

Arbenin: The end is pitiful;
              The start was beautiful!
              Please show me. The bracelet which is rather nice
              I may have seen somewhere twice.
              Hold on. It can't be so. I forget.

Zvezdich: How would I find her?

Arbenin: Why don't you try to get

Anyone of them: They're so many
                    Quite around!

Zvezdich: What if it's not her?

Arbenin: She may be easy to be found.
              It's not much trouble! With some devotion
              And fantasy . . .

Zvezdich: This bracelet may be helpful.
               I'll find her on the bottom of the ocean.

Arbenin: I hope she's is not an utter fool,
               And after two dance tours
               You will behold:
               Her track has long since grown cold.

Arbenin waiting for Nina (N. Kouzmin)

SCENE 3

SUBSCENE 1

(Yevgheniy Arbenin enters: a manservant is there)

Arbenin: Well, the party's over, and I'm glad,
              Though this rabble and this masquerade
                    Are spinning in my mind.
              It's time to put it all behind
              And to relax, at least, a minute.
                    Isn't that funny what I was doing there?
              Telling a paramour what is fair,
              Checking his guesses and enamelware . . .
              And dreaming for others, the way only poets practice.
              It's not for my age to be an apprentice!
                    (To the servant)
              Well, has my wife returned?

Ivan, Man Servant: No, Sir.

Arbenin: And when will she be here?

Ivan, Man Servant: She promised after eleven to return.

Arbenin: It's after one, and this is my concern.
              She might have stayed there for the night
              Until she sees the daylight.

Ivan, Man Servant: Sir, I don't know.

Arbenin: Indeed? Then you may go.
                She was expected here long ago.
                Please, put a candle on the table
                Should I need something, I'll be able
                To scream for you.

(The manservant leaves. Arbenin settles in his armchair.)

SUBSCENE 2

Arbenin *(alone)*: Oh, God is just; it is my doom
                To bear the woes of the gone-by days,
                For all my sins I have to face
                The ugly shadows of atonement gloom.
                There was a time I was awaited by others' wives,
                Today I have my own wife to wait . . .
                When in the circle of deceiving sweethearts
                I wasted all my youth on silly tarts.
                They all loved me with their flame and passion,
                From me not even did they have affection,
                Before I started an affair, I knew 'twas coming to
                a head,
                And, like a nursemaid, I would gladly spread
                For other hearts my fairytale
                Without fail.
                When life became both tedious and painful,
                I heard some wise advice
                To stop being wasteful,
                To marry someone
                And to find it wise
                To pay a sacred price
                For giving up all love for good.
                I found a submissive creature, a wife;
                I brought her to the altar, like a lamb of God,

And never in my life,
Indeed,
Did I see anything more beautiful,
And sweet . . .
But suddenly a sound from oblivion was awakened,
And when I into my deathly soul eyed,
I saw what got me terrified,
I must confess with shame . . .
My reawakened love for her was not forsaken!
It all came back the same:
Again my love, my dream,
Again the tempest rages freely in my empty breast,
A broken tiny bark flung into the sea of zest;
Shall I pick up my stream,
And get ashore and find my rest?
(Lost in thought)

SUBSCENE 3

(Arbenin and Nina)
(Nina tiptoes to the armchair and kisses her
husband's neck from the back.)

Arbenin:	Hello, Nina, you have come at last! It is high time.
Nina:	Am I too late?
Arbenin:	I've been waiting for, at least, an hour.
Nina:	Indeed? Oh, you're so sweet.
Arbenin:	You think he's a dolt, Waiting for me, and I . . .

Nina: Oh, my!
You always find someone at fault,
Always out of sorts and always with stern looks,
You pine for me when we're apart,
You grumble speaking heart to heart.
Why don't you tell me, "Nina,
Give up Beau Monde[10],
With you and for you I would want,
 To live,
Why should some soulless thief,
 A dandy of the streets, some baronet,
  Dressed in a tight corset,
From morn to eve should see you in Beau Monde,
While I, who is of you so fond,
May steal an hour during the day
A couple of words to you to say?"
Please tell me this, and I'm ready
To bury youth and to become a country lady.
I'd quit the ballroom, luxury and glamour
I'd bury boredom and my freedom's tremor . . .
Just tell me as a friend . . .
But where has me my imagination sent? . . .
Suppose you love . . . your love is so small
That knows not of jealousy at all!

Arbenin *(smiling)*: What can I do? I'm used to living carefree
     And jealousy's ridiculous to me.

Nina: Of course.

Arbenin: Are you being wrathful?

Nina: No, just thankful.

---

[10] "Beau Monde" (French): the world of top Russian aristocracy.

Arbenin: You're a little sad.

Nina: To tell the truth,
             I'm not glad
             To know you don't love me.

Arbenin: Nina?

Nina: What is it?

Arbenin: Look here Nina, we are fettered
             To share our fate for life.
             Perhaps, it was an error that predestined
                 You to be my wife.
             We are not able to pass the judgment.
             (He draws Nina to his lap and kisses her)
             Young is your soul, and so is your age.
             You've read only the title page
             In the enormous book of life,
             Into the sea of happiness and evil
                 You may dive,
             And you may choose your own way
                 Of hope and dreams.
             There is so much hope far away
                 And so chaste is your past life!
             You gave your whole self to me
             Without knowing my heart or yours,
                 I do believe you're in love with me,
             Frisking around, like a child, and you traverse
             Instinctively your playful feelings.
             I love you in my own course:
                 I went through all,
                     I know it all,
                 I realized it all.
             I often loved, more often hated.
             My sufferings never abated!

At first I wanted to have all,
Then held all in contempt.
The world and I in understanding
    Were so much incongruent.
So many years elapsed unending,
And on my life I had
A big seal of damnation,
My earthly joys were sad,
My cold unfolding feeling had no revelation . . .
I feel a deep revulsion
About those days of my perverted youth,
Excitement poisoned with convulsion;
    I always feel so uncouth,
When I reflect while resting on your breast.
Oh, what a wretch I was! Your worth and role
    I could not know . . .
But soon this dried-up bark
    Stripped off my callous soul;
For beauty of the world my eyesight was augmented,
    And not in vain,
For life and goodness I was resurrected.
But sometimes it is some evil Spirit
    That carries me away
Into the turmoil of my stormy past . . .
    My memory gets overcast . . .
The evil Spirit makes them sway:
The magic of your voice,
The radiant look,
The heavy burden of the thoughts I took,
    When struggling with myself,
    Into myself I delve,
Becoming silent, grim, and stern,
    And fearing to defile you
        With my touch or groan,
Wrenched out by my suffering,
    And then I hear your muttering

"He does not love me!"
(She is stroking his hair and looking at
him with caress)

Nina: You are a weird man! . . . When you with so much
            expression,
            Are telling me about love,
            Your thought is shining in your eyes with passion,
                    And above
                Your head is all on fire.
                Then I believe without concession,
                But often . . .

Arbenin: Often?

Nina: No, but at times . . .

Arbenin: You're too young, I'm too old at heart,
            But our feelings shouldn't go apart.
            And at your age, as I remember, in my past
            My trust in everything was very fast.

Nina: Angry again . . . My God!!

Arbenin: Oh, no . . . I'm happy, happy and insane,
            I'm a cruel slanderer. Let's forget the pain
            Of dark and heavy older days,
            So far from cross and envious crowd.
                I'm happy having you around,
                To witness how God repays
                By sending you to me from heaven.
            (He kisses her hands and fails to see her bracelet.
            He stops and gets pale.)

Nina: You're pale, you're trembling . . . Oh, my God!

Arbenin *(jumping up)*: I! No! Where is your other bracelet?

Nina: Lost.

Arbenin: Ah! Lost.

Nina: Well, it may have cost
               Twenty-five roubles at the most.
               So what? It's not a great disaster . . .

Arbenin *(to himself)*: Lost . . . this bracelet is a blaster
               That whispers me a weird suspicion!
               What an embarrassment! Was that only a dream?
               Is this awakening a real vision? . . .

Nina: What you're saying is beyond my comprehension.
               Arbenin *(folding his hands, with a piercing look)*:
               The bracelet lost?

Nina *(offended)*: To lie to you is my intention.

Arbenin *(to himself)*:   But likeness, likeness!

Nina: I must have dropped it in the coach.
                    Tell them to search with care.
               Had I imagined this reproach,
                    I wouldn't dare to wear . . .

SUBSCENE 4

(Arbenin rings the bell and the manservant walks in)

Arbenin *(to the manservant)*: Please search the coach and all over:
                    A bracelet is lost there . . .
               And God forbid you dare

Not to bring it over!
My happiness and honor are at stake.
(The manservant leaves.
Arbenin, after a short pause, to Nina)
What if the coach is a grave mistake?

Nina: Then,
            I must have lost it in another place.

Arbenin: Another? Do you know where?

Nina: You've never been so stingy and unfair.
            To quickly reassure you
            I'll promptly order one brand-new.
            (The manservant reenters)

Arbenin: Well, answer me at once!

Ivan, Manservant: I had to search the coach all over.

Arbenin: And have not found it!

Ivan, Manservant: No, the search is over.

Arbenin: I knew it . . . You may go.
            (Giving Nina a significant glance)

Ivan, Manservant: It may so happen
            At the masquerade
                'Twas lost.

Arbenin: Ah! . . . Masquerade! . . . So you were there?

SUBSCENE 5

(The same people, except for the manservant)

Arbenin *(To the manservant)*: You may go.
(To Nina)
Wouldn't that be fair
To tell me in advance, and I'm certain, Ma'm[11]
You would have granted me the honor
To graciously escort you there and back.
Strict supervision wouldn't be in excess,
    Nor would I bring you to distress
        With vulgar, trivial caress.
Who was with you?

Nina: It is the people's due
To tell you all and even more,
Item by item, whom I kept the bracelet for,
And you will know better hundredfold,
As if yourself you saw the fancy ball.
(She laughs)
My God, I'm amused, amused,
    But you should be ashamed
    It is a sin to get inflamed
        Over a trifle.

Arbenin: Oh, let your laughter not be stifled
Unless, God willing, it is last!

Nina: It will not, certainly be last,
Unless your gibberish has passed.

---

[11]   From here Arbenin, though inconsistently, uses very formal pronouns toward his wife. They, in this translation, correspond to "Ma'm" and "Mrs."

Arbenin: Who knows it . . . maybe . . .
Look here, Nina!
Of course, it's so ludicrous of me
To love you dearly,
      Intensely and infinitely,
            As granted to a human sinner . . .
And how strange? Some other people in the world
Enjoy a million hopes and aspirations,
Some in the wealth their point unfold,
      Some seek in science approbation.
Some people strive for crosses, ranks or fame;
Some seek Beau Monde to get inflamed;
Some need to travel; others gamble,
      And their blood is boiling . . .
I travelled and I played, was frivolous, was toiling,
I've learned to understand my friends,
      The treachery of love,
I did not strive for ranks, nor did I get my fame,
      Wealthy or penniless,
            Weary of boredom, all the same . . .
      I saw the evil everywhere
And always proud, nowhere
      Did I bend my knee
              In its behalf.
What's left for me from life
Is you, my beauty angel and my wife,
      A fragile creature . . .
With your love, your breath, your glance,
      Your smile, your features,
      As long as they are mine,
      I'm a human, I'm fine.
Without them I'm deprived of happiness and soul,
      Of feelings
      And of living!
But if I'm deceived . . . deceived . . .,

If on my breast the Serpent has been warming,
    If lulled to sleep, I was relieved,
    What kind of truth is forming
    For so many days,
    The truth by guess,
    And ridiculed by someone else
    Behind my back,
            while I was dreaming in caress.
    Oh, hear me, Nina . . . with a lava stream
    Of sizzling heart,
            That's how I was born.
    Like rock, it's always hard.
            It cannot melt or turn
    Into . . . It is an evil dream
    For people to confront this stream!
            Do not expect forgiveness then,
                I won't call in the law
                when . . .
            I, without tears or regret,
                Shall   by   myself   my
                vengeance let
            Your life and mine tear to pieces!
*(He wants to take her by the hand, but she cringes
back in fear)*

Nina: Do not come near . . . Oh, how terrible you look!

Arbenin: Oh, is that so, my Mrs. *(misses)*?
            Terrible? You must be joking. I'm absurd and
            cannot spook!
            Do laugh and laugh at me . . .
            Why should you blanch and tremble with horror
                When you have finally attained the aura
            Of fiery love? And where is he,
            Your plaything of the masquerade?

All other hellish torments which are made
You let me taste; so let him come and have some fun:
    Another torture to be done.

Nina: Oh, what a horrible suspicion!
The only culprit is this sole bracelet,
Oh, please believe your supposition
Will be laughed off by the Beau Monde,
    Not only I, myself, the whole world
    Is going to laugh and to regret!

Arbenin: You laugh at me
                You, all the morons of the world,
      You laugh, light-hearted, miserable
                    Husbands,
    This is what I am here to unfold:
There was a time I, too, deceived you
               In abundance.
You, husbands, think you live in paradise and well . . .
Alas . . . My paradise is you, in heaven and on earth . . .
                  Farewell!
Fare you well . . . I know everything.
(To her)
You get away from me, hyena!
A fool, I thought that this czarina[12],
Moved by my emotions,
Shall open me her heart and kneel
With sadness and remorse . . .
I would, then, softer feel
Should I have seen a tear, one only tear . . .
But no! Laughter is the only thing I hear.

Nina: I do not know who could vilify.
But to console you, I'll, certainly, not lie.

---

[12]   czarina: Queen (Russian); Pronounced "tsareena"

And I forgive you. I feel no shame.
And I'm sorry I can't help you in this game.

Arbenin: Be silent!
                I beg you . . . It's enough!

Nina: Oh, hear me, Yevgheniy. I do love you!
                May the Almighty punish me,
                If I'm not innocent. Please, listen . . .

Arbenin: What are you going to tell me from the heart,
                    I've learned it off by heart.

Nina: It does pain me to hear your reproach.
                Yevgheniy, I do love you.

Arbenin: Upon your word, it's time to broach
                Your true confession, Nina.

Nina: And I'm begging you again to listen . . .
                My goodness! What are you going to arrange?

Arbenin: Revenge!

Nina: Revenge? On whom?

Arbenin: Who knows what may happen in due time.

Nina: Revenge on me? Go ahead!

Arbenin: A stance of heroism you should not set.

Nina *(with contempt)*: Revenge on whom?

Arbenin: Whom do you fear for?

Nina: Oh, stop it . . . this jealousy of yours
       Is killing me . . . You're unyielding . . .
       There is no appeal of mine that stirs
       Your heart and I cannot appeal,
       But nonetheless, I pardon you.

Arbenin: Spare your effort!

Nina: Yes, God is here. He will not forgive you.

Arbenin: Sorry for you.

       (Nina leaves in tears)
       (Arbenin alone)
       Here's the woman! . . . Oh, I've known you all,
       All your reproaches and caresses,
       And for the wretched knowledge one possesses,
       How dearly one pays the toll!
       And, indeed, what should I be loved for?
       Is it for my stern looks and formidable voice!

       (He approaches his wife's door and listens).
       What is she doing? Would laughter be her choice?
       No, she is crying.
       (While leaving)
                      Sorry, she should have cried before!

                      End of Act I

ACT 2

Baroness Strahl (N. Kouzmin)

SCENE 1

SUBSCENE 1

*(The Baroness, tired, sits in an arm chair.
She throws her book away.)*

Baroness:

Just think of it: what do we live for?
Is it to always please a stranger we abhor?
And to remain enslaved? What is the woman for?
A plaything for his passions? A whim in the man's sight?
George Sand is almost right![13]
A thing without will and action.
Her judge is, certainly, Beau Monde,
And yet, to her protection
It is not going to respond.
Auctioned for sale from youth -
- a human sacrifice is not uncouth!
She has to mystify the flames of her emotions
Or stifle them in their full bloom . . .
"Guilty" of loving solely herself,
She's barred from loving other people.
At times her breast stirs up a storm of passions in itself,
The storm that chases reasoning and fear to belittle,
And when one day, neglecting power of Beau Monde,

---

[13]   George Sand (French pronunciation: "Zhorzh Sand") was an outstanding female French writer of the 19th century who bore a male pen name and wore a man's attire to symbolize emancipation. The author of "Lelia".

She would unveil her feelings,
Surrender to the man she's fond,
Then, she'd bid farewell to happiness and calm!
Beau Monde is here, and it doesn't want to know
Your secrets! It, by your palm and balm,
Will tell an honor from a vice, and so,
Beau Monde, to keep decorum,
Is very cruel in its forum!
                    (She wants to read)
No, I cannot read . . .
                    I'm bemused,
                    And feel confused
By what I thought and did.
I fear him as if he were a foe . . .
I marvel at my way,
When I recall
What happened on that day.
(Nina enters the room)

SUBSCENE 2

Nina: While riding out in the sleigh,
             I thought it might be good to pay
             This visit, mon amour.[14]

Baroness: C'est une idee charmante, vous en avez toujours![15]
             (they sit down)
             Despite that wind and frost today,
             You look unusually pale.
                         I bet
             It's not of tears that your eyes are red?

---

[14] Mon amour (French): my love
[15] A great (charming) idea, as is always with you (French).

Nina: I am not well today,
              All night I tossed in bed.

Baroness: Your doctor's bad.
              Why don't you take another?

Subscene 3

Prince Zvezdich enters the room.

Baroness: *(coldly)* Ah, Prince!

Zvezdich: I brought the news to you last night
              That our picnic had been canceled.

Baroness: Be seated, Prince.

Zvezdich: I have just bet
              That you'll be upset,
              But you don't seem to worry.

Baroness: I *am* really sorry . . .

Zvezdich: And I'm even glad:
              And I would trade
              Some twenty picnics
              For a masquerade.

Nina: A masquerade? Were you there last night?

Zvezdich: I was.

Baroness: In what disguise? *(laughing)*

Nina: There were so many . . .

Zvezdich: Yes, some ladies love to be disguised,
And some were easy to identify,
With their masks, in their guise.

Baroness: *(with some heat)*
I must declare, Prince,
That for a decent lady to decide
To see all kinds of riff-raff
Your aspirations aren't funny at all,
To go where honor is at risk to fall;
When she's recognized by any silly jerk
Whose aim is only to insult, to mock.
Renounce the statement, Prince, and be ashamed.

Zvezdich: Renounce? No. But I feel ashamed.

(A clerk enters the room)

SUBSCENE 4

(Same people and the clerk)

Baroness: Where're you coming from?

Clerk: Right from the Management.
I've come to talk your business over.

Baroness: Have you already reached its settlement?

Clerk: Not yet, but soon it'll be over.
Am I, perhaps, disturbing you?

Baroness: Not in the least.
(She steps aside to the window and talks)

Zvezdich: *(to the side):* This is the time for explanations.
              (to Nina): I've just seen you in a shoppe.

Nina: In which one?

Zvezdich: In an English one.

Nina: And how long ago?

Zvezdich: Just now.

Nina: I didn't recognize you, and I wonder why?

Zvezdich: I saw you busy going to buy . . .

Nina: *(quickly)* Choosing a bracelet for a match
              For this one here *(she takes a bracelet out of her purse)*
              From an entire batch . . .

Zvezdich: It is a pretty bracelet, but where is the other?

Nina: Lost!

Zvezdich: Indeed?

Nina: I lost it. Yes, I did.
              What's so special about it?

Zvezdich: And when? Is that a secret?

Nina: Maybe, last week, or yesterday, the day before,
              Why should you know when?

Zvezdich: I had my own idea then,
              A weird one, perhaps.
              (To the side)

My question has embarrassed her.
Oh, these modest ladies!
(To her)
I want to offer you my help . . .
The bracelet could be found.

Nina: You're most welcome to . . .
But where do we go around?

Zvezdich: And where was it lost?

Nina: I can't recall.

Zvezdich: Was that, perhaps, some fancy ball?

Nina: Quite possible.

Zvezdich: Or was it given for a keepsake?

Nina: Who would I give it for a keepsake to?
My husband? Why is that conclusion?

Zvezdich: It isn't my illusion
That in the whole world
There's just your husband.
No doubt, you have a whole host of lady friends . . .
Suppose it is lost;
Whoever finds it
May or may not get a reward?

Nina: *(smiling)* Depends . . .

Zvezdich: But if he loves you,
If he finds in you,
The dream he lost,
If for your smile and word,

He spares nothing in the world,
   If ever you become so bold
To give a hint of future bliss,
   If you, yourself,
Under a mask, unrecognized,
Caress him with the word of love
Please, understand . . .

Nina: I only comprehend
From all of this:
You got carried away too far.
I humbly beg you not to speak to me,
The first and last time.

Zvezdich: Oh, my!
I dreamt. You're really enraged?
(To himself)
Got rid of me? All right . . .
The time will come,
And I shall win my fight.
(Nina comes up to Baroness. The clerk bows down and leaves.)

Nina: Adieu, Ma Chere[16], it's time to leave.
See you tomorrow.

Baroness: Oh, no, mon ange[17], we had no time
To say two words.
(They kiss each other)

Nina: *(leaving)* I'm expecting you tomorrow morning.

---

[16] Adieu (French): goodbye
Ma Chere (French): my dear
[17] Mon ange (French): my angel

(She leaves)

Baroness: The coming day seems longer than a week.

SUBSCENE 5

(The same people, except for Nina and the clerk)

Zvezdich: *(to the side)* You'll be avenged, my modest lady!
              She may deny the bracelet,
              And I may be a moron,
              But I recognized it.

Baroness: Are you engrossed in thought, my Prince?

Zvezdich: Oh, so many things are called to mind.

Baroness: It seems you've had a lively conversation.
              What was the subject of your disputation?

Zvezdich: I claimed I'd seen her at the masquerade.

Baroness: Whom?

Zvezdich: Her.

Baroness: Wow, Nina?

Zvezdich: Yes.
              And I've proven it to her.

Baroness: I see you as a shameless
              Talking scandal, man.

Zvezdich: Out of weirdness, I sometimes dare . . .

Baroness: Be merciful, at least, behind our backs!

                 You said you had the proof, but where?

Zvezdich: No . . . But yesterday
                 I did receive a bracelet from some dame,
                 And Nina has precisely the same.

Baroness: Oh, what a proof! . . . A logical reply!
                 They carry them in any shop!

Zvezdich: Today in all of them I've stopped,
                 And I'm sure two such bracelets only
                         Will make the whole supply.

                 (After some silence)

Baroness: Not later than tomorrow
                 I'll give Nina some useful advice:
                 Not to confide in chatterboxes.

Zvezdich: And what advice is there for me?

Baroness: For you it would be wise
                 To go ahead with it more boldly,
                 To value honor of the women who are worldly.

Zvezdich: For your two pieces of advice
                 I thank you doubly.
                 (He leaves)

SUBSCENE 6

Baroness: The woman's honor is a thoughtless joke!
                 And I would, too, become his target,

If I removed my cloak!
Farewell, my Prince, not I shall lead
You from the path of error.
Oh, no, God forbid.
And yet, I cannot puzzle out
That it's *her* bracelet that I found.
Yes, Nina went to the masquerade,
And that's the clue to the charade.
I do love him, and I don't know why.
Perhaps, out of boredom, out of frustration,
Out of jealousy; burnt with agitation . . .
No, nothing brings me exultation!
As if I heard the laughter
Of those silly crowding rats
And hear the whisper
Of those spiteful regrets!
No, I must see myself
Even at somebody's expense,
And at the price of my torments,
I'll save myself from this disgrace . . .
This new misdeed of mine and disrepute
Will have to be made good!
(*deep in thought*)
Oh, what a chain of horrible events!

Subscene 7

(*Sprich enters and bows down*)

Baroness: Ah, Sprich, you always come in time.

Sprich: Indeed, it would be fine
              To be somehow helpful to you.
              Your deceased spouse . . .

Baroness: Don't you ever grouse?

Sprich: Blessed be the Baron's memory . . .

Baroness: Some five years back
              As far as I remember . . .

Sprich: He borrowed some money.

Baroness: Yes, I am aware.
              And you'll get today what's fair:
              Your five year interest.

Sprich: I do not need it now at all,
              I merely by chance recall.

Baroness: Tell me what's new?

Sprich: Beau Monde is overflown with its stories.
              I have just left a Count's house
              And heard them all.

Baroness: And did you hear of Nina and Prince Zvezdich?

Sprich: No . . . Yes, I did . . . Oh, no . . .
              (Perplexedly) Beau Monde has talked
                      And stopped . . .
              (To the side): What was that all?
                      It's terrible: I can't recall!

Baroness: Well, if the story's so well spread,
              Then, there's nothing to be said.

Sprich: But I'd like to know your judgment, Baroness,
                      In all its fairness.

Baroness: They've been condemned by the Beau Monde,
             But I could still with some advice respond.
             I would advise the prince to be persistent;
             This value makes a woman less resistant.
             The woman wants a man to find his way
             Through thousands of bars that may
             Appear on his way,
             To reach his icon.
             And I would wish her less severity
             But modesty far more!
             Goodbye, then, Monsieur Sprich,
             My sister is expecting me for lunch,
             But otherwise,
             I'd be glad to stay with you for more.
             (To the side while leaving)
             It was a useful lesson which has saved my soul.

SUBSCENE 8

Sprich: *(alone)* Oh, don't you worry:
             Your hint is understood!
             And an intrigue is there . . .
             I do not think I could
             Wait more for repetitions!
             And what a game of a sophisticated mind!
             I won't be sorry, if I find
             This secret link.
             I even think
             The Prince will thank me as his agent.
             Then I'll rush back with my report,
             And for the word I brought
             I shall, perhaps, receive
             My five year interest.

SCENE 2

SUBSCENE 1

*(Arbenin's study room.
Arbenin alone, later with a servant)*

Arbenin: My jealousy accepts it,
              My mind has no proof.
              I fear to err,
              But cannot take it longer
              To keep my dignity aloof.
              To let it drop as something no stronger
              Than the forgotten momentary slip?
              This life is more horrendous than a grave!
              I saw the people who may sleep,
              With their souls cooled,
              And for the state of peace they crave,
              The bliss of peace
                        In weather storms . . .
              An enviable life!

Servant: *(entering)* There's someone waiting downstairs.
              He brought my barynya[18] a note
              From some Princess.

Arbenin: From which one?

Servant: I haven't worked it out.

---

[18]   Barynya (Russian): of 'BARYN (masculine): a wife of a Russian
       nobleman as referred to by servants.

Arbenin: The note? For Nina?
(He is leaving. The servant remains here.)

Subscene 2

(Afanassiy Pavlovich Kazarin and the servant.)

Servant: Baryn[19] has just stepped out.
Please wait . . . a little.

Kazarin: All right.

Servant: I'll report at once.

(He leaves)

Kazarin: Monsieur[20] Arbenin, I'll see you once,
Ready to wait a year, if needed to.
It saddens me to feel the misery of my affairs!
A very clever friend is needed.
It wouldn't be bad, if he became the one who cares
Quite lavishly, quite often, and, by the way,
Along with patronage in the nobility, he may
Possess some three thousand serfs.
It would be good
To draw Arbenin
Back into the game;
He'd be faithful just the same
As in the old days.
He'd be able to support a friend,

---

[19] Baryn (Russian): "master" toward a servant in the 19th century aristocratic families.

[20] Monsieur (French): the way to address to a Russian nobleman (Mister).

He wouldn't fear any "child" who plays,
　　To tell the truth,
　　This modern youth
　　Just stabs me in the heart!
　　　They do not know
　　　How to stir to action
　　　　　Or when to stop.
　　　Nor do they know
　　On what occasion honesty to show
　　　Or when to honorably cheat!
　　Look at the older men and what they did!
By gambling many got their ranks
　　And rose from the mud,
To the nobility they sent their thanks,
　　And why is that?
The new decorum was to be maintained,
　　The law in anything—to be observed,
The rules for every single thing—to be abided by.
And now look! They keep their millions
　　　　　And their honor!

SUBSCENE 3

(Kazarin and Sprich.
Sprich enters)

Sprich:　　Ah! Afanassiy Pavlovich,
　　　　　What a surprise!
　　　　　So glad to meet you here.

Kazarin:　Likewise.
　　　　　Are you on a visit, dear?

Sprich:　　I am. And you?

Kazarin: So am I!

Sprich: Indeed?
              And a good thing we did
              That you and I got here together:
              We'll discuss a certain affair.

Kazarin: Isn't it your first time that you dare
              To really discuss a business instead of some affair?

Sprich: Bon mot[21] is not exactly to the point:
              But we're in the same boat.

Kazarin: And here's my important point:
              I also want to speak to you.

Sprich: Then our effort could be joined.

Kazarin: Don't know . . . What is on your mind?

Sprich: If I may ask you,
              Didn't you hear
              Arbenin, a friend of yours, is so blind
              That . . . (Sprich makes horns with his fingers)

Kazarin: Oh, no!
              It can't be so!
              Are you sure?

Sprich: My God. I smoothed things over by myself
              Some five minutes ago.
              Who else is here to know?

Kazarin: The devil is again around.

---

[21]   Bon mot (French): a good (witty) word.

Sprich: You see, his wife has found
           A certain little Prince,
           I don't remember where—
           In church or in the ballroom
           Or at the masquerade somewhere;
           It was the other day.
           She gave him ample time to look at her,
           And soon enough
           The Prince found himself in love
           And happy,
           But suddenly the beauty tried to escape . . .
           The Prince, then, went berserk,
           Flying around everywhere;
           Now his stories really irk
           His listeners: the trouble is around the corner!
           They asked me to be prompt to settle the affair,
           I took it up and made it fair.
           The Prince, then, promised to keep quiet
           And wrote a careless note,
           Your humble servant made a slight correction
           And started off in this direction.

Kazarin: See that her spouse doesn't do you ear resection.

Sprich: I handled very serious affairs,
           But managed to avoid duels.

Kazarin: And weren't you even beaten up?

Sprich: It's all a joke and a laugh to you,
           And I always contend
           You mustn't risk your life
           Without any purpose.

Kazarin: And such a priceless life!
           To risk it? Such a sin, indeed!

	We all would lose Its priceless use.
Sprich:	Put it aside. It's an important deed That I would like to speak about.
Kazarin:	What is this?
Sprich:	An anecdote, and this is what it's all about:
Kazarin:	Take your affairs and get lost. It seems Arbenin is coming up.
Sprich:	No, nobody's there. From Count Vrutti They brought me five greyhounds, breed "borzoi".
Kazarin:	Your story is really funny.
Sprich:	Your brother is a hunter. Buying the dogs he would enjoy.
Kazarin:	So, Arbenin's like a fool.
Sprich:	Please, listen.
Kazarin:	Exposed to ridicule, Deceived and taken in, Marriage? Oh, no! Not after that!
Sprich:	Your brother would be glad To come across a find like that.
Kazarin:	The married folks say That they are faithful and happy. It's only their way

To lie!
Hey, don't get married, Sprich!

Sprich: It has been long since I received this pleasure.
Look here! One is a real treasure.

Kazarin: A wife?

Sprich: A hound.

Kazarin: Oh, these dogs are your obsession!
Look here,
Sprich, my dear,
God knows if a given wife pays off;
As to your dogs,
Not soon enough will you be able
To sell them off.
(Arbenin enters with a letter in his hands, without
seeing Kazarin and Sprich who stand by the desk)
That letter buries him in thought:
I wonder what's in it.

Subscene 4

(The same characters plus Arbenin)

Arbenin: *(without seeing the others)*
Oh, human gratitude! And wasn't that long ago
That I did save his honor and his future,
While I did hardly know
What he was like . . . Alas, you, snake!
Unheard of baseness! This man,
Toying with me, intrudes my house, like a thief,
Who covers me in shame
And even with disgrace!

And I did not believe my own eyes,
Forgetting all bitter experience of many days.
Like an inexperienced child,
I thought it was her fault . . .
That he was unaware
Of who that woman was.
I did not even dare
To suspect the crime of such a kind.
I hoped he would forget
That night adventure,
Like a weird dream!
And yet,
   He didn't forget . . .
He sought and found, and then he couldn't
   Stop his venture . . .
Oh, human gratitude! Yes, I did see the world,
   But still keep wondering.

(He rereads the letter)

"I've found you,
But you did not
Admit the truth".
—His modesty is quite amazing—
"You're so right. The wicked rumor is uncouth.
We might be overheard by chance.
I read just fear in your ardent eyes,
And not contempt. No, you do not despise.
But you love secrets, and the secret it shall be!
The loss of you would be the death of me".

Sprich: The letter! Yes, this is it. It's done! It's just like that.

Arbenin: Hey! You, artful tempter!
    You really deserve a bloody answer.
    (to Kazarin)

Ah, were you here?

Kazarin:	I've been waiting for, at least, an hour.

Sprich: *(to the side)* I shall be seeing Baroness,
And be it in her power
She may possess,
She'll make a fuss over the mess.
(He approaches the door)

SUBSCENE 5

(The same people minus Sprich)
(Sprich leaves unnoticed)

Kazarin: Sprich and I . . . Where's Sprich?
Gone.
(to the side)

The letter! Just like that! I see!
(to Arbenin)
You're deep in thought . . .

Arbenin: Yes, I'm in contemplation.

Kazarin: You're in thoughtful observation
Of frailty of hopes and earthly good.

Arbenin: Close to it! Of human gratitude.

Kazarin: It is still worthy of some meditation,
Though on that account
There's a lot of differentiation
In points of view.

Arbenin: And what is your opinion?

Kazarin: I think, my dear friend,
That gratitude may well depend
On costs of favors,
That goodness isn't quite a blend
With our volition.
For instance, Slukin lost me
Five thousand last night;
So, I'm thankful to him,
And this is right,
And when I sleep or eat or drink,
About him I always think.

Arbenin: You're still joking, Kazarin.

Kazarin: Look here, brother, with all of my affection,
I'll speak in earnest,
But, please, do me a favor:
Abandon all of your stern looks,
And I'll disclose those earthly wisdom spooks.
You want to know
What I think of gratitude . . .
Well, here we go:
Just be patient.
Whatever they may say,
Voltaire or great Descartes[22]
To me—the world is just a deck of cards.
Life is the bank,
Fate runs a deal,
And when I play,
    I feel
For people—my own rules of game
Are pretty much the same.

---

[22]   Descartes (French philosopher): pronounced [De'cart]

And here is a sample of clarification:
Suppose once I put a thousand on an ace.
Just out of premonition
In cards I see an ill omen!
Suppose, by chance, without deception,
That ace has won.
I am not going to thank that ace;
In silence, I will be raking in
                My gain.
Then, I'll keep on playing, playing, playing,
Until exhausted I will sum it up
And throw that last and only crumpled card
Under the table! And then, my dear fellow,
You're not listening to me?

Arbenin: (in thought) Evil is all around,
Deceit is everywhere,
But I, without a single sound,
And in stupor, attended
What it was the other day!

Kazarin: *(aside)* His mind is wandering.
(to Arbenin): Let's now take another case
And slowly figure out
                Without
Getting off the track.
Say, for example, you're back,
      Up to the neck,
In gambling or in a debauch,
And here is a friend of yours
Who would say,
"Hey, brother, watch!"
And other worthless pieces of advice
From someone who is "wise".
And then, you'd casually follow his advice
And bow him down and wish eternal life,

And if you're stopped from drinking by this punk,
Without delay, please, make him drunk,
And beat him in the game
Exchanging for his good direction,
And if from gambling you got his protection,
Then take and love his dame!
Or, if you aren't in love, seduce his wife
To pay her husband back this way.
In both cases, you're right, my friend,
One lesson with another to repay.

Arbenin: You are some moralist.
            (aside)
            So the rumor's spread . . .
            Hey, Prince . . . The lesson I've had
            Shall fairly be repaid.

Kazarin: *(heedlessly)*
            There's the last point I would explain:
            Do not expect a woman's gratitude in vain . . .
            You love a woman, and you sacrifice
            Your friendship, wealth, your life, maybe;
                    You sacrifice
                    Full price
            Out of passion, and, perhaps, self-love,
            You lavish her with fun and flattery,
            You do it only to possess her,
            But not to make her happy.
            And now think of it in cold blood,
            And say yourself a word
            That all is arbitrary in this world.

Arbenin: *(downcast)* Yes, yes, you're right:
            What does a woman seek in love?
            She needs new conquests every day.
                    You may,

Perhaps, torment yourself, and cry, and pray,
Just funny are your face and tearful tone,
Yes, you're right:
He is a fool who dreams to find
     His earthly paradise in her alone.

Kazarin: Hey, for a happy married pal
              You truly reason very well.

Arbenin: Indeed?

Kazarin: And am I wrong?

Arbenin: Oh, I've been happy so long . . .

Kazarin: I am pleased to hear it.
              Yet, sorry you're married!

Arbenin: But why?

Kazarin: Well, I remember our past . . .
              When you and I would go on a spree
              At someone else's place and in full blast.
              We, both chums with our good heads,
              Had lots of fun when we were great and free . . .
              The morning of a gentle rest,
              The recollections of a pleasant night time,
              Then dinner and wines—in Raul's honor—
              Foaming and sparkling in faceted goblets,
              And rousing talks, and countless jests,
              And then, a theater!
              My soul now shivers at the thought
              How you and I did our best
              With those lady dancers
              In order to entice them from behind the wings!
              Isn't that true that in the early day

All was much better and cheaper than today?
And when the play was over,
We'd fly,
Straight as an arrow,
To a friend's,
And we would go in,
And see the game in its full swing . . .
The cards hold
Mounds of gold,
This gambler would be all on fire,
Another one is paler than a corpse . . .
We would sit down, and a battle
        Would flare up its course!
And it is now, now that a thousand passions
        And sensations
Would through your soul run,
And often an enormous thought would wind
The starting spree in an ardent mind . . .
And if you beat a gambler with savoir faire[23],
Then you would find it fair
        To force the fate itself
To humbly fall down at your feet.
Then even Napoleon himself
Would seem both silly and absurd.

(Arbenin turns away)

Arbenin: Oh, those stormy hopes, come back to me!
Where are you those unbearably ardent days?
I would give up my unconcern and rest,
My blissful ignorance and zest . . .
No, those are not my ways
To have a family, to be a spouse,
It is not what I was meant to be!

---

[23]   Savoir faire (French): ability to do the right thing. Pron: [savuə fair]

I who has tasted every sweetness
Of vice and villainy
Without ever trembling!
Abandon me, oh, virtue:
I know you not!
Even you, virtue, have betrayed me,
And I'm breaking
My brief union with you!
Farewell, farewell to you!

(He falls into a chair and covers his face)

Kazarin: He is now mine!

SCENE 3

(A room in Prince Zvezdich's house.
The door is ajar. In this room Zvezdich sleeps on a couch.)

SUBSCENE 1

(Ivan, a man-servant. Later—Arbenin.
The man-servant looks at the clock)

Ivan (*a man-servant*): It is well after seven now.
He ordered to awaken him at eight.
He doesn't follow the fashion
And sleeps the Russian way.
Then I can make it for the store,
And lock the door:
Safer this way.
But hold it! Someone's walking
Up the stairs.
I'll say nobody's home:
Quicker that way.
(Arbenin enters the room)

Arbenin: Is your master in?

Ivan: No, Sir. He isn't in.

Arbenin: *(listens up)* You, liar! He's in.
(He points at the study room)
And he is sleeping like a log!
You can hear his breath.
(aside)

I'll put an end to that . . .

Ivan: *(aside)* He's got sharp ears.
           (to Arbenin) My master didn't want to be awakened.

Arbenin: He loves to sleep.
           So much the better:
           One day he won't be awakened.
           (to Ivan) It seems I said
           I'd be waiting
           Until he rouses from his sleep!
           (Ivan leaves)

Subscene 2

Arbenin: *(alone)* What an auspicious moment! Now or never . . .
           I'll accomplish all without any effort and without fear
           I want to prove that if in my generation ever
           One single soul insulted may appear,
           If the abuse is lodged, it bears fruit . . .
           It is too late to bow down to them,
           And I am not their servant.
           If I were to scream
           And challenge my foe to his face,
           Then they would laugh.
           No laughter anymore!
           Oh, no. I'm not that kind . . .
           I shall not tolerate even one hour of disgrace
           Over my head, for nothing.

           (He opens the door)

           He is sleeping!
           What is his dream about in this last sleep?

(with a terrifying smile)

I think he'll die by a single stroke—
—He's hanging his head—
I'll simply help his red
        Blood soak
And let the wholesome nature make him dead.

(He enters the room)
(After *some two minutes, he comes back pale)*

No, I can't!
(Silence)
No, it's beyond my will and power.
I have betrayed myself, and I've trembled
The first time in my life.
Did I become a coward?
How long ago?
A coward? I?
Who said that?
I did, and I spoke the truth . . .
Oh, how shameful, shameful!
Then you deserve your own contempt,
You, run and blush!
The times have crushed
You, like the others, to the earth;
And, how pitiful, oh, pitiful you seemed,
When you were only bragging to yourself,
When under pressure of enlightenment
You have fainted and collapsed.
To love? You've failed to love . . .
To take revenge?
You wanted to avenge,
You came and failed again!
(silence)
(he sits down)

I've flown too high,
And I must choose to rectify my path.
Another plan has now sunk deep
Into my broken heart.
Yes, yes, this man shall live!
Murderers are not in fashion anymore;
They face a public execution.
Yes, I was born in an enlightened nation:
Instead of our daggers and our poison
We've got our gold and tongue in store!
(He writes a message in ink and picks up his hat)

Arbenin confronts Baroness Strahl (N. Kouzmin)

Subscene 3

(Arbenin and the Baroness.
In the doorway, Arbenin runs into a lady in a veil)

Lady: Ah! All is ruined!

Arbenin: What is that?

Lady: *(with a sudden outburst)* Let go of me!

Arbenin: No, that wasn't a pretended cry of easy virtue.
             (severely to her)
             Silence!
             Not a word, or else this minute . . .
             What a suspicion! Take off your veil,
             While no one else is near.

Lady: It's the wrong door. I'm mistaken to be here.

Arbenin: And wrong you are . . . a little,
             So it seems,
             About time, but not the place.

Lady: For Heaven's sake, I've never seen your face.

Arbenin: Well, your embarrassment is weird,
             You must confess
             You've got the right address . . .
             He's asleep but may awaken now!
             Knowing all, I want to make it certain how . . .

Lady: You know everything!

(He throws off her veil and steps back in amazement.
Then he regains his composure)

Arbenin: Thanks Heaven, I am wrong this time.

Baroness: This is my end. Oh, what's my crime?

Arbenin: Your desperation's out of place.
              It is unpleasant, I admit, to face,
              At such a time, a cold hand,
              Instead of craving
              For a passionate embrace!
              There is no other harm
              Than this momentous shock . . .
              You may, perhaps, thank God:
              I'm discreet, glad to keep quiet,
              Thank God that this is I,
              And not another man . . .
              If not, it would be a big noise
              Around town.

Baroness: He's awakened,
              And I heard him talking.

Arbenin: He's just raving in his sleep.
                    Calm down, I'm on my way,
              But please explain what power
              This Cupid has to have bewitched you
              And why all women are so ardently attracted
              To the man who is unfeeling,
              Like a piece of metal?
              And tell me why
              It is not he who's at your feet
              With longing, pleading, vows, and tears?
              Why is it you, alone here, a lady with a soul,

Who came
Forgetting any shame,
In order to surrender
Without any fears?
Why is another woman,
In no way worse than you,
Prepared to give away to him
Her happiness, her life, her love . . .
For just one glance, one word?
Why? What a fool I am!
(In his fury)
Why? Why?

Baroness: *(with determination)*
I understand what you have talked about.
I know that you have come . . .

Arbenin: What? Who on earth has told you that?
(regaining his composure)
What do you know?

Baroness: Oh, forgive me. I implore you . . .

Arbenin: No, I did not accuse you.
I, on the contrary,
Am glad
The Prince is happy

Baroness: I was just blinded by passion,
It's all my fault, but listen . . .

Arbenin: What for? It's all the same to me.

I challenge strict morality.

Baroness:	But if it hadn't been for me,
	There would be no letter,
	Nor would . . .
Arbenin:	Ah, that is too much of a good thing!
	A letter? What kind of letter?
	Ah, so it was you!
	You brought and taught them . . .
	How long ago did you take up this business?
	What forced you to?
	Do you trick sinless victims to this place
	Or do young people visit you?
	I must admit you're a real parlor treasure,
	And the depravity of our women's pleasure
	Does not surprise me anymore!
Baroness:	Ah, goodness gracious!
Arbenin:	I do not flatter you.
	How much money do you earn?
Baroness:	*(sinking back into the chair)*
	But you are a beast!
Arbenin:	Oh, I'm wrong and sorry.
	You serve out of honor.
	(he starts out)
Baroness:	I'm going out of my mind.
	Wait! He's leaving.
	He won't listen . . .
	Oh, I'm dying . . .
Arbenin:	Well, please continue,
	You'll reach your glory . . .

Today don't fear me, and fare you well!
But God forbid
To meet
Again.
You took away from me all I can tell,
I shall forever stalk you everywhere,
In town, in solitude, and in Beau Monde,
And if we ever clash, you face distress!
I would be glad to murder you, but death
Is a reward I must reserve for someone else.
You see, my dear, I am nice:
Instead of agonies of hell,
You'll enjoy the earthly paradise.
(He exits)

Subscene 4

*(Baroness alone.
Following Arbenin)*

Please, listen! I can swear
That it was my deceit . . .
She's innocent; as to the bracelet there,
It's I, it's I who is to take the heat!
He's gone . . . He wouldn't hear,
What can I do? There is despair
                    Everywhere . . .
No need
For it . . .
Whatever looks as fit
I'll employ to save his life.
I will expose my crime and my deceit,
I'll beg and make my disposition bend,
But he awoke. He's coming . . . It's decided.
Oh, torment!

SUBSCENE 5

Baroness and Zvezdich.

Zvezdich: *(from the next room)* Ivan! Who's there?
             I've heard some voices!
             What kind of folks are there?
             They wouldn't let me take a nap,
             Not even for half an hour!
             (He enters the room)
             Say, what a visit!
             A beauty? I am, indeed, rejoiced.
             (then he recognizes her and steps back)
             Ah, Baroness! No, it's inconceivable.

Baroness: Why are you jumping back?
             (in a weak voice)
             Are you amazed?

Zvezdich: Of course, it's so amiable . . .
             (embarrassed) I didn't expect it so good.

Baroness: It would be most weird, if you did.

Zvezdich: Oh, had I known it, I would . . .
             What did I think about?

Baroness: You could have known everything,
             But did know nothing.

Zvezdich: It is my fault, but I'm ready to make it good.
             And with humility shall I accept my punishment
             Of any kind . . .
             Oh, I was dumb and blind.
             It is my ignorance,
             Which was at fault,

Words fail me to express . . .
(he takes her by the hand)
Your hands, your hands . . . Ice cold!
I see much suffering
In your face
Do you doubt
My words and ways?

Baroness: How wrong you are! I did decide
To visit you, casting aside
My shame and fear,
And all those things so dear
To all of us.
I came not for demands of love
And not for begging your confessions.
I came out of sacred obligations:
My past is gone,
I face a different life . . .
I was the cause of evil.
Before I leave Beau Monde for good,
I came to make it good
For the past life!
I'm prepared to bear my shame,
I've failed to save my own good name,
But I'll save another . . .

Zvezdich: What does it mean?

Baroness: Please do not interrupt me!
It took me courage to speak out . . .
You, alone, although being out,
Caused all my sufferings.
In spite of them, it's up to me
To save your life . . . Why and what for?
I do not know. You do not deserve
This sacrifice, you could not love

Or understand me, and, perhaps,
I wouldn't have wished your love.
But listen! I've learned today,
Never mind how, that yesterday
You thoughtlessly wrote a letter
To Arbenin's wife . . . And rumor has it
That she loves you, but it's false, it's false!
For heaven's sake,
Do not believe it!
This very thought is fake.
The thought alone may ruin us all!
She isn't aware,
But her husband *read*!
And in his love and hate he's mad!
He's been here . . . And he'll murder you.
He has been trained to be a villain,
But you're so young . . .

Zvezdich: You fear in vain!
Arbenin isn't insane.
He knows Beau Monde well,
And he won't dare tell
His secret and make a bloody end,
Without any need or purpose,
In this prepost'rous comedy.
But should he really explode,
I wouldn't see much trouble in it.
We'd measure off thirty-two feet,
And then, we would unload
Our pistols of Lepage[24].
It's not by fleeing from the enemy
I earned these epaulets.

Baroness: But if your life is dearer to someone else

---

[24]   Lapage (French name). Pronounced [le'pazh]

Than it's to you . . .
And if it's tied in with someone else's,
If you get killed . . . Killed! Oh, God forbid!
And that would be my fault and all my deed.

Zvezdich: Yours?

Baroness: Have mercy on me.

Zvezdich: *(pondering for a moment)*
I must fight.
I've hurt his honor,
Although I didn't mean to,
But there is no way to justify.

Baroness: Yes, there is just one.

Zvezdich: Is it to lie? Find me another one.
To lie—to save my life is not the way,
I'm already on my way.

Baroness: Please, wait a moment! Do not go.
Listen! *(She takes him by the hand)*
You're all deceived . . .
That mask was I!

Zvezdich: You?
Oh, Providence! *(Silence)*
But Sprich! He said . . . It's all his fault . . .

Baroness: *(recovering from her shock)*
It was a momentary bolt
From the blue, a weird madness,
And now I repent!
It's passed. Forget it all.

Return the wretched bracelet to Nina.
By some strange fate
'twas found.
Please, promise me to keep this secret;
Of me alone, God will be the judge.
He shall forgive you,
And you're not at will to forgive me!
Let me retire.
I do not think we'll ever meet again.
(in the doorway, seeing that he wants to follow her)
Do not follow me.
(Exits)

SUBSCENE 6

(Prince Zvezdich, alone)

Zvezdich: *(after long musing)*
I really don't know what to think of that,
And yet,
Of all of that
I only can collect
That, like an immature lad,
I've missed my lucky bet
And failed to act.
(He comes up to his desk)
Well, here is a note . . . From whom?
Arbenin . . . I'll read!
"My dear Prince,
Please visit N. tonight,
There'll be a lot of going on there,
And we'll have a good time . . .
I did not want to waken you,
Or you would be dozing off all evening.

Please, do come.
         Yours truly,
         Yevgheniy Arbenin".
Well, it takes a special eye
To read in this "cartel."[25]
Who would, on earth,
Invite to dinner
Before he called
         To a duel?

---

[25] "cartel" and "duel", for the purpose of rhyming, are pronounced here with the stress on the last syllable. "cartel", in the poet's era, meant "written challenge to duel".

Arbenin Accuses Zvezdich of cheating (N. Kouzmin)

SCENE 4

(A room at the N's)

SUBSCENE 1

(The host, Kazarin and Arbenin sit down to play)

Kazarin: In fact, you've quit all those fancies,
On which Beau Monde so prides itself,
You've touched again the path of chances!
The thought is brilliant! You, yourself,
Must be a poet, and, moreover,
A genius, by every indication.
Domestic life brings no pacification.
Give me your hand,
My dear friend.
You're with us.

Arbenin: I *am* with you! The past leaves no trace.

Kazarin: It's nice to witness how, by God's grace,
Smart people now look upon the world,
Proprieties to them are worse than chains,
And wouldn't it be too bold
To ask to go half with me?

Host: We'll have to fleece the Prince a bit.

Kazarin: Oh, yes! *(aside)* The clash will be a bit of fun.

Host: Oh, we shall see. I hear the carriage!
                 (some noise is heard)

Arbenin: This is he.

Kazarin: Is it your hand that trembles?

Arbenin: Never mind. I've been out of practice.
                 (Prince Zvezdich enters)

SUBSCENE 2

(Zvezdich and the others)

Host: Ah, Prince! I'm very pleased.
                 Don't stand on ceremony,
                 Take off your saber, and sit down.
                 A frightful battle's burning here.

Zvezdich: I'm prepared to watch.

Arbenin: And playing cards do you still fear?

Zvezdich: Not really. Not when you're near.
                 (aside)
                 To the rules of the Beau Monde
                 I am ready to respond:
                 I should oblige the husband,
                 While I run after his wife . . .
                 I'd better win there and lose here!
                 (He sits down)

Arbenin: I have visited you, Prince.

Zvezdich: I read your note,
             And you can see me here.

Arbenin: On your threshold
             I encountered someone,
             Embarrassed and alarmed.

Zvezdich: And did you recognize that someone?

Arbenin: *(with laughter)* I think I did, my Prince.
             You are a treacherous seducer.
             I understood, I figured out all . . .

Zvezdich: *(aside)* It's clear he didn't understand at all.
             (he steps aside and lays down his saber)

Arbenin: I wouldn't want you
             To take a fancy to my wife.

Zvezdich: *(absentmindedly)* Why not?

Arbenin: Well, I do not possess the virtue
             Lovers may seek in husbands.
             (aside)
             He does not feel embarrassed. Not at all . . .
             I shall destroy
             Your sweet, sweet world,
             My stupid boy,
             And I would add to it my poison.
             If on a card you staked your soul,
             Then I would put mine on a dole.
             (They play and Arbenin deals)

Kazarin: I'm putting down fifty roubles.

Zvezdich: So am I.

Arbenin: Here's a funny story
I heard when I was young,
The story I can't throw out of my mind.
You see, a barin,
—You're doing well, Kazarin—
So, that married man,
He trusted totally his wife
In his sweet unconcern—
—You're too much concerned,
My Prince, and you'll lose like that—
The nice beloved man,
The carefree husband,
He lived just day by day, in peace . . .
And, to top off his bliss,
The husband had a friend.
An important favor
The husband did
To that devoted friend of his;
It seemed the friend repaid
With dignity and honor.
So what! Who knows by what trick of fate
The husband learned
His thankful friend and his too honest debtor
Took a fancy to his wife . . .

Zvezdich: And what did that husband do?

Arbenin: My Prince, do not forget the game.
You're playing without looking.
(looking at Zvezdich fixedly)
So, you are curious to know
What her husband did?
He picked some minor pretext
And slapped his foe
In the face . . .
And you, my Prince?

	If you were in his place, What would you do?
Zvezdich:	I would do the same. And later? Did they square off with pistols?
Arbenin:	No.
Zvezdich:	Did they fight with swords?
Arbenin:	No, no.
Kazarin:	Did they make up then?
Arbenin:	*(smiling bitterly)* Oh, no.
Zvezdich:	And so, What did he do?
Arbenin:	The husband was avenged, And closed the case, And left his foe With that slap in the face.
Zvezdich:	(laughing) But that is quite against the code.
Arbenin:	The code? Where is the code To unfold the mode? Or a rule to hate? Or how to avenge? *(They play on in silence)* And that one takes it . . . I win. Hold on, I saw you switch that card.
Zvezdich:	I? Look here . . .

Arbenin: The game is ended,
            And the decency is over.
            (out of breath)
            You're a scoundrel and a cheat.

Zvezdich: I? I?

Arbenin: Yes, a scoundrel,
            And I'm marking you right here,
            And everyone who happens to be near
            Will take offense just meeting you.
            (Arbenin throws the cards in the Prince's face.
            Zvezdich is so appalled that he does not know what
            to do)
            (Arbenin, lowering his voice)
            We're even now.

Kazarin: What's wrong with you?
            (to the Host)
            He broke it up in the best place,
            The Prince was mad, ready to lose, at least, Two
            Hundred Thousand.

Zvezdich: *(coming to his senses, jumps up)*
            It is my turn, my turn is now
            To wash away your insult with your blood.

Arbenin: Exchange our shots? With you? For me?
            You are deluding yourself, Prince.

Zvezdich: You are a coward!
            (He is about to throw himself at Arbenin)

Arbenin: *(sternly)* Go ahead!
            But I do not advise you
            To assault me

Or even to remain here.
You couldn't scare even a coward,
If I were that coward!

Zvezdich: Oh, I shall make you fight!
I'll tell everywhere what you did,
And everyone will know
That *you* are a scoundrel, not I!

Arbenin: For that I am prepared.

Zvezdich: *(coming up nearer)*
I'll say I was with your wife.
Don't you forget the bracelet,
Be on your guard!

Arbenin: For that alone you are punished hard . . .

Zvezdich: Oh, my rage! Where on earth am I?
The whole world's against me,
I shall murder you!

Arbenin: And that is in your power to decide,
I'll even dignify you with advice
To kill me quickly. It'll be wise
Before your courage may run cold
Within an hour.

Zvezdich: Where are you, my honor!
Take back your word,
Give up what you just did,
And you'll find me at your feet.
What do you hold as sacred?
Are you a human or a demon?

Arbenin: I? A gambler!

Zvezdich: *(falling and covering his face)*
             Oh, my honor!

Arbenin: No, your honor won't return.
             The whole Beau Monde, with scorn,
             Is going to turn
             Its back on you.
             The barrier has been removed
             Between the evil side and good.
             And outcast's is now your only way,
             The happiness of others is going to weigh
             Upon your soul.
             The sweetness of your bloody tears
             You shall taste . . . And night and day
             You'll be thinking of the same.
             And gradually
             Your sentiments of love and beauty
             Shall fade away,
             And die . . .
             No art shall give you any pleasure,
             And at leisure,
             Your joyous friends will, certainly, drop off,
             Like leaves fall from a rotten branch,
             And you'll blush and hide your face,
             While walking through the crowd,
             And shame shall gnaw at you,
             Stronger than a crime does
             At an accomplished villain!
             (leaving the room)
             I wish you a long life!
             (He exits)

END OF ACT 2

ACT 3

SCENE 1

(A Ball)

SUBSCENE 1

Hostess:	I've been waiting for the Baroness,
	But, I'm sorry, in this mess
	I'm not sure she's arriving.
	I would be sorry for you,
	If she were not.

First Guest: I do not understand . . .

Second Guest: Are you expecting Baroness Strahl here?
Oh, she is gone. She is not near.

Other Guests: Has she been gone
long?
Why?
Where is she gone?

Second Guest: This morning she has disappeared,
Left for the country.

Lady: Good heavens!
What is it that made her go?
Left on her own free will?

Second Guest: It was some fantasy . . . romance or so.
Who knows what it was?

(They leave)
(A group of male guests appears)

Third Guest: Prince Zvezdich lost the game,

you know?

Fourth Guest: You are wrong here. He has won.
Yet, clearly, he's used some weird ways,
And in the end, his partner slapped him in the face.

Fifth Guest: And did he square off with pistols?

Fourth Guest: No, he declined.

Third Guest: Oh, what a scoundrel he must be!

Fifth Guest: From now on,
I'll set my mind
To know him no more.

Sixth Guest: And so shall I!
What a despicable way to act!

Fourth Guest: Will he come here?

Third Guest: I do not think he'll dare.

Fourth Guest: But look! He is already there!

(Zvezdich comes up. They barely bow down to him.
Then all but Fifth and Sixth Guests step out.
Later Fifth and Sixth Guests also step out.
Nina sits down on a settee)

Zvezdich: We are now apart from the crowd,

There'll be no other chance.
(To Nina)
You must, Nina, hear me out.
I must say two words at once.

Nina: Must I?

Zvezdich: Yes, for your own happiness.

Nina: Oh, how strange is your concern.

Zvezdich: It's strange because my ruin is your fault,
Because you, Nina, can't discern
                    What I can clearly see:
I am the victim of the same assault,
            And, Nina, I do pity you
Because the hand which struck me
                    Is going to kill you.
            I won't stoop to any insignificant revenge.
I'll wait . . . My day shall come, and I'll be avenged!
            Be, Nina, on your guard
And hear me out:
Without any doubt,
Your spouse is evil, heartless, godless . . .
            I have my premonition:
            Your trouble is quite near.
            Farewell forever!
                    The villain is still here.
            I cannot punish him.
                    Please take your bracelet back.
            I do not need it anymore.

(Arbenin watches them from a distance)

Nina: Because you're going out of your mind
My indignation has declined.

Zvezdich: Fare thee well forever, Nina,
              And I'm begging you again . . .

Nina: Where are you going, Prince?
              Not to the moon, of course?

Zvezdich: Much closer, to the Caucasus[26].

              (He leaves)

Hostess: *(to the guests)*
              Almost everyone is down here,
              And we shall need more space, I fear.
              Please step into the ballroom, gentlemen!
              Mesdames[27], please, follow the men.

              (She leaves)

SUBSCENE 2

Arbenin: *(alone)*
              Was I in doubt? I?
              The whole Beau Monde does know I'm a fool.
              These caustic hints are persecuting me . . .
              Oh, how I am ridiculed,
              And I'm so pitiful!
              And how are my efforts being returned?

---

[26]   (the) Caucasus: the Caucasian Mountains, or the South of Russia; typically, a zone of warfare with the local minority rebels. The Russian officers, including M. Lermontov himself, would spend some time fighting with the minority warriors and would demonstrate Russian valor. In his poetry Lermontov romanticized the Caucasus and its peoples.

[27]   Mesdames (French): Ladies. French was widely used by the 19th century Russian nobility.

And where is that power
Which more than once has turned
Against a crowd
To execute it
With one witticism, one word?
That power has been killed
By those two women!
One of them . . . Oh, I do love her!
I love,
And I'm so treacherously betrayed . . .
No! Not for the others she was made
The others shall not judge us!
I, myself, shall find her Judgment Day
To execute her in my own way . . .
But as for me, I shall be executed here.
(He points out at his heart)
Yes, she **must** die.
With her I cannot further live.
To live apart?
(As if frightened by himself)
So, it is settled.
Yes, she *shall* die.
The hardened heart
Of my past life
Shall never be betrayed.
It looks,
Like she is fated
To perish in the prime of life,
Fated to be loved by me, a villain,
Fated to fall in love with someone else . . .
Yes, it is clear
She cannot live with it around and near!
You, the Almighty, the Invisible,
But seeing all,
Take her, do take
Your due from me . . .

Bless and forgive her
The way
God only may!
I can't forgive: I'm not God!
(The sound of music is heard)
(He walks up and down, then stops)
Some ten years back
I was just stepping
Upon a life of dissipation.
On one unfortunate occasion
I lost all of my money in the game,
And I was broke within one night.
I was then able to unfold
The real cost of gold;
The price of life I couldn't name,
So I left in desperation,
Bought poison . . .
In my heart
My blood was boiling in vexation,
Into the gaming table I returned . . .
In one hand
I held a glass of lemonade,
And in the other
I held the four of spades.
And in my pocket
My last rouble[28].
Together with the cherished powder of poison
They patiently awaited their turn . . .
And then I took my risky chance
And almost at once
I managed to return,
All of the money lost.
My fortune smiled on me again!
Since then

---

[28] Rouble: Russia's currency.

Amid calamities of life
I have been saving
My cherished dusted "knife",
My talisman.
I saved it for a rainy day . . .
That rainy day is no longer far away.
(He leaves quickly)

Subscene 3

(The Hostess, Nina, several ladies and gentlemen)

(They all enter while Arbenin speaking the last 2 to 3 lines of his monologue)

Hostess: It wouldn't be bad to have some rest.

Lady: *(to the other lady)* It's so stuffy: I can melt.

Petrov: It would be best,
             If Nina sang us something.

Nina: The old romance has bored me,
             And I feel
             I haven't learned the new ones.

Lady: Indeed, Nastasya Pavlovna,
             Please, sing for us.

Hostess: You are too kind
             To have us beg you
             For so long in vain.

Nina: *(sits down at the piano)*
             Only to set you straight,

To ascertain
That I have no talents,
As punishment
I order you
To listen with attention!
(She sings)

When in your eyes I see
A casual fleeting tear,
Your sorrow doesn't pain my knee:
You're not happy with your other dear.
A hidden worm is calmly gnawing
Your fragile, tender life . . .
And as to me, to me, it's not annoying
To feel his weaker love will not survive.
Yet, when your radiant eyes may show
A sudden, unexpected fest,
Then, in a secret bitterness, I know
The flames of hell torment my breast.

SUBSCENE 4:

(The guests and Arbenin)
*(At the end of the third couplet, Arbenin enters and
leans against the piano. At seeing him, Nina stops singing.)*

Arbenin: Well, why don't you go on?

Nina: What is the end?
              I can't recall.

Arbenin: I'll remind you, if you want.

Nina: *(embarrassed)*
              Oh, no. Why?

> *(To the Hostess)*
> I'm not feeling very well.
> *(She rises)*

First Guest: *(to the second one)*
                    The lady of Beau Monde
                    Cannot deliver any fashionable song
                    With those vulgar words in it.

Second Guest: Yes, our mother tongue is too direct,
                    And women's whims it can't protect.

Third Guest: You're right:
                    Our proud language won't bend,
                    Just like a freedom-loving savage.
                    But WE, from our height,
                    Good-naturedly, WE bend
                    To our heart's content.

(Ice cream is being served. All the guests are walking up to the end of the ballroom and singly going into the other rooms. Finally Arbenin and Nina remain alone. A Stranger appears upstage)

Nina: *(to the Hostess)*
                    It's so stuffy in here.
                    I shall step away to rest.
                    (to her husband)
                    My Angel, I would love some ice cream.

> *(Arbenin shudders, goes for the ice cream,*
> *returns, and puts his poison into it)*

Arbenin: *(aside)* Oh, help me, death.

Nina: *(to him)* I feel so bored. I've lost my zest.
                    Misfortune is, of course, ahead.

Arbenin:	*(aside)* I sometimes trust my premonitions. *(Giving her the ice cream)* This is your antidote for boredom.
Nina:	Yes, it will cool me off.
Arbenin:	Oh, it *shall* cool you off Without fail.
Nina:	It's now so boring here.
Arbenin:	Not to be bored by people who are near, You'll have to look and learn, How cunningness and follies turn To make Beau Monde go around.
Nina:	It's horrible, and you're so right!
Arbenin:	Yes, horrible. That's right.
Nina:	And I have never found Any unsullied souls.
Arbenin:	No. And yet, I thought I'd found Just one unsullied soul, But I was wrong.
Nina:	What is it all about?
Arbenin:	I said in the Beau Monde I'd found One such a soul, 'twas you.
Nina:	You're pale.
Arbenin:	I danced a lot.

Nina: Oh, no, mon ami[29]!
          You've never left your seat.

Arbenin: So, I must be pale
          Because I danced only a little bit.

Nina: *(returning her empty saucer)*
          Here, please put it on the table.

Arbenin: *(taking the saucer)*
          All, all of it!
          Isn't it cruel not to leave
          One single drop for me?
          (Lost in thought)
          I have just made this fatal step,
          And it's too far to go back.
          This saucer shall not be the trap
          To die for her.
          (He throws the saucer onto the floor and breaks it)

Nina: Oh, how clumsy!

Arbenin: Never mind that. I'm falling ill.
          Please hurry up. We're going home.

Nina: Yes, we are.
          Today you're so sullen,
          Please, tell me, darling,
          Are you not pleased with me today?

Arbenin: Not really. Today
          I **have** been pleased with you.

          (They leave)

---

[29]   Mon ami: (French) my friend

Stranger: *(alone)*
              I barely gave in . . .
              There was a moment
              When I restrained myself
              From rushing forward . . .
              (He muses)
              No, let the destiny define its course.
              My turn will come, when I unfold my force.
              (He leaves)

SCENE 2

Subscene 1

(Arbenin's bedroom)

(Nina enters, her maid follows)

Maid: You look, ma'am, rather pale.

Nina: *(removing her earrings)*
That's right. I'm not quite well.

Maid: You must be tired.

Nina: *(aside)*
It was my husband whom I feared,
I do not know why!
While he's calm, his gaze is weird.
(To her maid)
I cannot breathe: it must be my corset . . .
Please, tell me . . . Was I smartly dressed?
(She approaches the mirror)
Yes, you are right: I'm pale like death.
Yet,
Who isn't really pale in Petersburg?
Perhaps, just that old Princess:
But it's all rouge,
It's all Beau Monde's pretense!
(She removes her curlers and fastens her braid)
Please throw them somewhere
And let me have my shawl.

(She sits down in an armchair)
Oh, how I loved that beautiful new waltz!
I whirled around and around in some rapture,
Faster and faster . . .
My mind and heart were magically captured,
And willy-nilly carried me afar . . .
And then my spirits sank . . .
More with some sadness,
And then they changed to gladness . . .
Please, Sasha[30], give my book to me.
And now, that Prince, with his "catastrophe" . . .
What was he raving in his clouded mind?
Was it "a villain" of some kind?
"A punishment?" "The Caucasus?" Such nonsense!
I pity him. This boy does make me feel upset.

Maid: *(pointing at Nina's attire)*
Is it all set?
And shall I put it all away?

Nina: No, leave it here.
(She becomes lost in thought)
(Arbenin appears in the doorway)

Maid: Am I to go?

Arbenin: *(to the maid, in a husky voice)*
Please, go.
(The maid does not move)
Do go.
(She leaves. He locks the door)

---

[30]   Sasha (pron. "SAHSHA"): diminutive of "Alexandra", a female or
male name in Russia.

SUBSCENE 2

Arbenin and Nina.

Arbenin: Do you still need her?

Nina: Are you here?

Arbenin: Yes, I'm here.

Nina: It seems I'm falling ill. Please, do come near.
            My head's on fire.
            Give me your hand: it's burning . . .
            Do you feel?
            Why did I eat my ice cream there?
            Oh, that is where
            I caught cold. Don't you think so?

Arbenin: *(absently)*
            Your ice cream?
            Yes, quite so . . .

Nina: I want to talk to you, my dear!
            Because you've lately changed;
            Your sweetness of caress is no longer here . . .
            Instead, I hear
            Your husky voice
            And meet your cold look.
            I know that the masquerade became the 'spook'.
            From now on,
            I hate them all,
            And I have sworn
            To never go there.

Arbenin: *(aside)*
              No fear!
              You will no longer dare!

Nina: Only one time I wasn't cautious,
              And then I had to pay my debt.

Arbenin: Not cautious? Oh!

Nina: That was the whole trouble.

Arbenin: You should have thought it over in advance.

Nina: Ah, if beforehand
              I had known your ways,
              I wouldn't have been your wife.
              To torture you and suffer many days . . .
              Oh, what a nice and joyous life!

Arbenin: Indeed,
              My love
              You do not need!

Nina: What kind of love?
              Who needs this kind of life?

Arbenin: *(sits down near her)*
              You're so right! And what is life?
              It's something meaningless.
              As long as blood is running swiftly in your heart,
              The world may bring you pleasure and delight,
              And then desires flit and passions dart,
              And light is turning into night!
              So, what is life?
              It is a trivial charade
              For children's exercises made:

Step one is birth, step two—a chain
Of ugly troubles, hidden wounds that pain,
And death comes last . . .
A whole life is lived in vain!

Nina: *(pointing to her breast)* Something is burning here.

Arbenin: *(continues)*
It's nothing! It'll pass!
Hush . . . Hear me out:
I say that life is precious
As long as it is beautiful . . .
But how long?
Yet, life is only, like a ball:
Around and around you may whirl
And have your fun . . .
And see the clear light of sun.
You come back home then,
And with your rumpled clothes off,
Your mind takes off all recollections,
Only fatigue does overcome you . . .
It is much better
To bid goodbye to life
Early in life,
Before the soul becomes akin
To life's so heartless void,
To instantly fly over
To the other world,
Before one's mind
Gets loaded with the past,
As long as struggle with death is easy . . .
Yet,
Only if you are fortunate
To have that fate.

Nina: Oh, no, I do want to live.

Arbenin: What for?

Nina: Yevgheniy, I'm suff'ring. I'm ill.

Arbenin: But aren't there other hurts that kill
            Much stronger, more severe?

Nina: Call for a doctor, dear.

Arbenin: Death is momentary,
            Life is eternal!

Nina: But I . . . I want to live.

Arbenin: And so many comforts
            Await the martyrs.

Nina: *(frightened)*
            I'm beseeching you:
            Send for the doctor now!

Arbenin: *(coldly and rising)*
            No, I shall not help you.

Nina: *(after a pause)*
            Of course, you're joking,
            But that's a godless joke:
            Send for the doctor now!
            I may die.

Arbenin: Well, Nina, can't you die
            Without the doctor?

Nina: Yevgheniy, you're a villain,
                  I am your wife.

Arbenin: Yes, you ARE my wife.
                  I know, I know!

Nina: Oh, have mercy!
                  The flames of fire
                  Are burning all over my breast!
                  I am dying . . .

Arbenin: Not so soon. Not yet.
                  (He looks at his watch)
                  You still have half an hour.

Nina: You do not love me.

Arbenin: Why should I love you?
                  Because you put a living hell in me?
                  Oh, no! I'm glad, glad
                  That you're suffering. My God!
                  My God!
                  To love you? How do you dare?
                  You dare to demand my love?
                  Tell me, didn't I give you all my care?
                  And was the price for my caress
                  So fair?
                  And what is it that I expected of your love?
                  A welcomed look and a sweet smile . . .
                  And what I found is treachery, betrayal . . .
                  And how did you manage to betray
                  ME, only for a fool's kiss, me . . .
                  And so soon!
                  ME who, at a word,
                  Would give his heart away?

Nina: Oh, if I knew my fault, I would . . .

Arbenin: Hush up! Or I'll go insane!
             When will these torments leave me?

Nina: My bracelet was by Zvezdich found,
             Some slanderer fooled you around.

Arbenin: So, I was fooled around!
             Enough, I was mistaken!
             I dreamt of happiness . . .
             I meant to love and to believe again . . .
             The fatal hour, then, has come,
             And everything has passed,
             Like the delirium in illness!
             Perhaps, if in my hope I had had some trust,
             My heavenly dreams would have come true,
             And in my heart I would revive
             The bloom of old days . . .
             You, Nina, turned your face
             Away from it, you, you!
             Cry, Nina, cry! But what is it,
             A woman's tear?
             It's only water!
             When I, a MAN, was crying,
             It was of jealousy, of wrath,
             Of torments, and of shame.
             Yes, I **was** crying!
             What is the meaning of a man's tear?
             You do not know it, my dear!
             When a man cries, do not come near:
             Death then in his hands may rest,
             A flame of hell is burning in his breast.

Nina: *(kneels in tears and raises her arms to heaven)*
             God the Almighty, God in Heaven!

Oh, please, have mercy!
He would not listen, but You hear
And know everything!
You, the Almighty,
You shall clear me of guilt!

Arbenin: Please, stop! At least, don't lie to Him!

Nina: I am not lying.
I shall not violate
His sanctity
With the false plea,
He's entrusted with the sufferer's fate,
HE judges you and protects me.

Arbenin: *(walking up and down the room, with his folded hands)*
Nina, this is the time to pray:
In a few moments
You shall end your way . . .
The mystery for people will remain,
The way you passed away,
Until we shall obtain
HIS fair judgment on the Judgment Day.

Nina: What? To die? Right now? It can't be so.

Arbenin: *(laughing)*
I knew beforehand
It would be hard to go.

Nina: Death, death!
He's right.
The hell of fire in full blast
Is in my breast.

Arbenin: I gave you poison at the ball.

                (silence)

Nina: I don't believe you.
                No, in your soul
                You have a spark of goodness . . .
                Oh, you're laughing,
                But you're not a demon
                To murder me in cold blood
                And in the bloom of life . . .
                Don't turn away from me, Yevgheniy,
                My anguish must be cut.
                Oh, save me and dispel my fear . . .
                And look me in the eye!
                Please! Here, here! Yes!
                Your eyes are telling me my death!
                (She falls onto the chair and closes her eyes)

                (He approaches and kisses her)

Arbenin: Yes, you are going to die,
                And I am here to remain
                Alone and alone . . .
                And years and years will go by,
                I, too, one day shall die,
                Again,
                I'll repeat the same refrain:
                Alone and alone!
                What can be uglier than that?
                But you! Have no fear,
                The world of beauty is quite near,
                Your angels are already here,
                To carry you to the abode
                Of God.
                (He cries)

I love you, yes, I do, I do . . .
And if I could undo
What happened,
I'd leave it in oblivion
Because to vengeance
Here is my limit, Nina:
Your murderer is shedding tears,
Like a baby,
Over you.
(a pause)

Nina: *(bursts out and leaps up)*
Please, rush to the rescue here!
I'm dying of poison, poison . . .
I understand they do not hear . . .
You've been cautious: nobody is near . . .
You, murderer, remember:
Before I pass away
You have my curse for Judgment Day.

(She falls in the faint before reaching the door)

Arbenin: *(with bitter laughter)*
A curse? It's no use cursing me . . .
I've been cursed by God.
(He approaches her)
A miserable creature . . .
This punishment is out of proportion . . .
(He stands with his hands folded)
So pale!
(He shudders)
All of her features are at rest;
They show no repentance, no remorse . . .
What if she was . . .?

Nina: *(in a weak voice)*
      Yes, I'm dying innocent . . .
      Farewell, Yevgheniy!
      You are a villain . . .

Arbenin: No, no, do not speak like that!
      And rest assured
      The mystery of death will die with you!
      No lies, no cunning are going to help.
      Please, tell me: I was deceived . . .
      Even the hell itself can't joke with my love!
      Oh, you're silent! Silent?
      This is how my vengeance pays . . .

Nina: I do not care anymore . . .
      And I remain still innocent before HIM.
      (She dies)

Arbenin: *(comes up to her and then turns away immediately)*
      This is a lie!

      (He falls into the armchair)

End of Act Three

ACT 4

Arbenin faces the truth (N. Kouzmin)

SCENE 1

Subscene 1

(Arbenin sits on the couch by the table)

Arbenin: I struggled with myself.
And these torturous efforts
Have weakened me . . .
At last I taste
A kind of hard, deceptive peace!
Yet, sometimes some unwanted care
Disturbs my soul in its cold slumber,
And when my heart begins to ache,
I feel
There's another torment
Left for me to bear . . .
It seems not everything
Is coming to an end!
Rot! Days and days will pass
And slowly melt into oblivion,
The weight of years
Will kill imagination . . .
Then, in the final destination
An eagerly awaited peace will rest
In my unruly breast.
(He muses, then raises his head)
Oh, I was wrong!
How implacable
Is my recollection!
So vividly

> I see her pleading and her grieving . . .
> Oh, you, Serpent[31]! Pass by swiftly . . .
> Why
>   have I
>   awakened you?
> *(He drops his head on his hands)*

SUBSCENE 2

Kazarin: *(quietly)* Is Arbenin here?
Yes, sighing and sorrowful.
Let's see
How he plays at comedy.
(To him)
Mon Cher Ami[32],
I've hastened here
As soon as your misfortune
Touched my ear.
It can't be helped.
With everyone's afflictions,
We bow down to the fate's predictions.
(Pause)
Come on, my friend,
Don't pull this long-long face for me.
Remove your solemn looks,
These looks are good only for those
Who feel carefree . . .
But you and I are actors,
Not just spooks.
Please, tell me, brother . . .
Oh, how pale you are!
As if you've lost your game

---

[31]   Serpent: here "Satan" (origin "Bible", "Old Testament")
[32]   Mon Cher Ami (French): My dear friend

Over the night.
Aha, old rogue, we'll discuss it later. Right?
Here are your folks.
They came to pay respect to the deceased.
Goodbye, my friend.
We'll meet again whenever you please.
(He leaves)

SUBSCENE 3

(The relatives walk in)

Lady: (to her niece)
             It seems that the Lord's curse
             Is looming over him:
             A wicked husband, a malicious son.
             Remind, my dear, please,
             To buy me some material
             To dress for mourning.
             There's no more money left at all,
             But for you all
             I'm prepared
             To ruin myself.

Niece: Ma Tante[33], what is the reason
             My cousin passed away?

Lady: Beau Monde is in its silly fashionable season,
             With its misfortunes always underway.
             (Both ladies leave)

---

[33]   Ma tante (French): my auntie

SUBSCENE 4

(A doctor and an old man come out of the deceased's chamber)

Old Man: Were you, doctor, there when she died?

Doctor: I? No. Me? They didn't have the time to find.
    I've always said
    Ice cream and balls
    Make any trouble
       Doubled.

Old Man: The pall is rich.
    Have you examined the brocade?
    Last spring I had it made,
    Precisely the same one, for my brother's coffin.
    (He leaves)

SUBSCENE 5

(The doctor comes up to Arbenin and takes him by the hand)

Doctor: You have to rest.

Arbenin: *(shuddering)* Ah!
    (aside) It breaks my heart!

Doctor: You went through so much suffering last night.
    Please take a nap.

Arbenin: I'll try to.

Doctor: You cannot help her anymore. It would be right
    To take some care of yourself.

Arbenin: Oh, I'm indestructible.
              Whatever earthly suffering
              Has victimized my breast,
              I'm still alive . . .
              I longed for happiness,
              And then, a God-sent guest,
              An angel, came down to me.
              Alas, my foul breath
              Profaned its holiness,
              And here, look!
              This beautiful God's creature
              Is now cold and dead . . .
              Once in my life
              I put my dignity at stake
              And saved a stranger's life.
              I helped him to evade
              A wreck. But he, amid his jests and laughter,
              Without even saying just another word,
              He took away my world, my whole world,
              And just within an hour.
              (He leaves)

Doctor: I do not doubt he's seriously ill,
              A thousand torments are going through his head.
              He is already getting mad,
              And if he goes out of his mind,
                              Then I will find
              It is my duty,
                              At least, to answer for his life.
              (While leaving, he runs into two men)

SUBSCENE 6

Prince Zvezdich and a Stranger come in.

Stranger: May I request you if Arbenin could be seen?

Doctor: I wouldn't venture to say yes
In view of the condition he's been in:
His wife died yesterday.

Stranger: Sorry to hear that.

Doctor: And he is so upset.

Stranger: And I feel sorry for Arbenin.
Yet, is Arbenin in?

Doctor: Yes, he is in.

Stranger: I have a serious subject of concern.

Doctor: You, gentlemen, are, certainly, his friends?

Stranger: Not yet. But we came here to earn
His friendship . . . Little by little.

Doctor: He is seriously ill.

Zvezdich: *(frightened)* In bed? Unconscious?

Doctor: No. He walks and talks.
And I have hope still.

Zvezdich: Thank God!

(The doctor leaves)

SUBSCENE 7

Zvezdich: At last, it is, precisely, my hour!

Stranger: Your face is all on fire.
           And do you have the power
           To stick to your decision?

Zvezdich: Are you prepared, Sir, to bet
           That so just is your suspicion?

Stranger: Look here: the same target we have set,
           And both of us hate him.
           But you don't know his soul,
           Dismal and deep,
           Like the door to a tomb.
           Whatever it may open up to,
           Becomes the dole[34],
           Forever buried in his soul's womb.
           Yes, in his soul
           Proofs and suspicions merge,
           He knows not an urge
           To show any mercy, to forgive . . .
           And when the beast feels wounded,
           He does desire to avenge:
           Revenge! Revenge!
           That is his purpose and his law.
           This death was quick, and not without a cause . . .
           I knew you were his foe, and, of course,
           I would be glad
           To stand you in good stead.
           When you begin to fight,
           I'll step out to the right
           To be a witness of the scene.

---

[34]   Dole (archaic British): one's fate, sorrow, grief

Zvezdich: Yet, where have you been
                To find out
                He has insulted me?

Stranger: I would be glad
                To tell you that,
                But you'd be bored.
                Besides, the rumor's spread
                In the Beau Monde.

Zvezdich: It's an unbearable thought!

Stranger: And can't you take it easy?

Zvezdich: Oh, disgrace is something
                You didn't know of.

Stranger: Disgrace? No.
                With more experience
                You'll forget it.

Zvezdich: But who are you?

Stranger: You need my name?
                I'm your partner,
                And for your honor and your shame
                I'm standing up, all by myself,
                In all my earnestness,
                In all togetherness.
                Isn't that sufficient to know?
                But hush! His pace, heavy and slow,
                I can hear.
                It's him. No doubt he's here.
                Retire, Prince, just for a moment,
                And stay near.
                I have to see him face-to-face:

You should not witness our ways.
(Zvezdich steps aside)

Subscene 8

(Arbenin carrying a candle)

Arbenin: Death! Death!
The word is here,
And it's all over . . .
It's penetrated me,
It's permeated me . . .
The whole hour
I did stand to peer
At her mute corpse,
Bending my knee,
With not a word . . .
My heart became the world
Of anguish that I couldn't express . . .
I saw her childlike, carefree smile
Which bloomed so agile
And quietly,
With all her features so calm:
She hears her eternal psalm.
Eternity may read her soul's fate . . .
But was I wrong? No, here a mistake
I could not make.
And who would dare to tell me otherwise?
Yet, was she innocent? No, these are lies and lies.
I didn't believe HER, and whom should I believe?
I was a passionate husband;
As to a judge, I'm cold and fair.
And who is wise enough to dare
To prove me otherwise?

Stranger: I am that wise person to dare!

Arbenin: *(Frightened, he steps back to put his candle closer to
               the Stranger's face)*
               And who are you?

Stranger: No wonder you do not know me, Yevgheniy,
               Though we used to be good friends.

Arbenin: But who are you?

Stranger: I'm your good prevailing spirit.
               Yes, unnoticed. I stalked you everywhere,
               Always changing my face,
               Always in a new apparel clad,
               And always knowing
               All of your new ways,
               And sometimes even thoughts,
               And at the masquerade
               A warning I've made of late.

Arbenin: *(shuddering)* I don't like prophets.
               Please leave at once:
               I mean it.

Stranger: That is so.
               Despite your clear-cut order
               And your threatening voice,
               I'll give you no chance
               To hope I would leave at once:
               I SHALL NOT LEAVE.
               Yes, it is getting crystal-clear:
               To me you're turning a deaf ear.
               You do not recognize.
               At any moment of the danger

I'll never been that total wreck
To take a definite step back,
To turn away the dream
Of so many days,
To turn away my aim
Which I have reached,
And in this very place
I would rather die
Than go away.

Arbenin: I'm like that myself,
              But I don't boast about it.
              (He sits down)
              I'm listening to you.

Stranger: *(aside)* I haven't reached him so far.
              Am I then wrong about his "scar"?
              Let's see what happens.
              (To Arbenin)
              Arbenin, you used to know
              Me
              Some seven years ago.
              I was then young and inexperienced,
              Hot-headed, rich.
              And as to you,
              That chill already settled
              In your heart,
              That devilish contempt for everything,
              That scorn
              You flaunted everywhere!
              For me to understand your soul
              Is hard:
              Shall I attribute something to your brain
              Or to the facts of life in their chain,
              I do not know of it,

Because the secrets of your soul
Are understood by God alone,
For He, alone, is the Creator of your heart.

Arbenin: The "debut" sounds good.

Stranger: And the "finale" won't be any worse.
You talked me into it,
You sucked me in . . .
One day,
When, with my wallet full,
I sat down to play,
And played against you
All the way.
I did believe in luck,
But lost the game.
My dad was miserly and strict.
And to evade all shame,
I sat down again
To play.
But you, though young, you had me in your claw,
And then another game, again, was lost.
Yes, I gave way to my despair . . .
You may remember very well
My pleas and tears:
In response
I heard your laughter:
"I don't care!"
I would prefer a dagger
Stuck into my heart,
But at that time
You didn't use the art
Of prophecy. It's only now
That the evil seed
—I do not know how—
Produced the worthy fruit.

(Arbenin first wants to jump up, but then he moves)
And since that moment on,
I have abandoned the pursuit
Of happiness; I did abandon
Love and women,
The bliss of youth,
All these sweet longings,
And those tender dreams . . .
And then it seems
That in this world
Another world of light
Opened to me—
The world of new queer sensations,
The world of outcasts and icy revelations.
The world of proud souls
And fascinated torments.
Such was the world I saw . . .
The world of money which is the Czar[35] on Earth,
And I bowed down to that Czar.
Then years went by,
With health and riches gone,
In front of me, alone,
The door to happiness was locked.
Yet, there's one covenant with fate
I have already made.
I am what I AM now . . .
Oh, you tremble, you are afraid,
You understand my purpose,
And you know what I've said.
Tell me again
That you don't know me,
Please, go ahead!

Arbenin: Go away! I know you, I do!

---

[35]   Czar (or "Tsar", Russian): ceasar, king.

Stranger: Go away?
               Is that all you say?
               I was your laughing-stock,
               And now it's my turn to laugh.
               Quite recently I've heard the talk
               That you're married, rich, and happy,
               And I felt bitter, and my heart rebelled;
               And then I thought and thought:
               Is that a well-deserved reward?
               And something clearly whispered:
               "Go-go and distress,
               Go-go, and harass! "
               Then I began to stalk. I mingled with the crowd,
               Never tired . . . Always on your track,
               And always knowing what people talk about.
               At last my efforts have paid back.
               And now, please, listen:
               I have found out
               And I shall reveal one truth to you:
               (He draws out his words)
               Arbenin, Nina's murderer was you!

               (Arbenin jumps back. Prince Zvezdich comes up.)

Arbenin: I have murdered? I?
               Prince! Oh, what's going on . . .?

Stranger: *(stepping back)* Yes, he will go on,
               And I have said
               What I did have to say.

Arbenin: *(going insane)*
               Ah! A plot . . . That's fine . . .
               And I'm in your hands . . .
               And who, indeed, would dare to defy?
               No one. You're the masters here.

I'm quite humble, at your feet . . .
And who is it, indeed?
My soul gives way before your looks!
I haven't defence against your snooks.
So, I'm conquered instantly,
I'm deluded jokingly . . .
And peacefully I shall put my head under the axe.
Haven't you, gentlemen, discerned
That I'm in the presence of my mind,
And that my strength has not declined,
That my experience is something I can find,
That these things have not concerned
Her grave
Which has not taken what I earned?
Haven't you, two morons, thought
That in the same old-fashioned way,
Without any reservations, I shall pay
To both of you?
Is that how,
By artful rumors' prattle,
You thought
You brought
Me down?
When you were thinking this scene out,
Did you guess
What end was going to be about?
And this lad?
Did he decide to fight me?
This lad is always carefree,
And, yes, he prays
After receiving one slap in the face
To get another.
And yes, my dear, you'll get it all.
You are bored with life!
No wonder: it's a moron's life,
The life of a street corner Don Juan.

Please rest assured, I'm quite able to forestall
You shall be killed,
And yes,
You'll die a scoundrel's death.

Zvezdich: That *shall* be seen,
But hurry up.

Stranger: *(leaving the couch)*
Prince, you have dropped the bottom line!

Zvezdich: *(stopping Arbenin)*
Hold on. You must by now know
You have accused me falsely,
That INNOCENT your victim was,
That you insulted me in time . . .
I was about to disclose all to you.
Now let's go.

Arbenin: What? What?

Stranger: Your wife WAS innocent.
And as to you,
You were
Too harsh with her.

Arbenin: *(laughing)* You have a lot of jokes up your sleeve.

Zvezdich: I swear in the name of God
It's not a joke. No. You'd better believe:
By accident, the Baroness once got
Into possession of a bracelet.
And from her own hand
I then received the bracelet for a keepsake.
Yes, I was wrong myself:
Your wife resented my desire . . .

Had I known
That only one mistake
Would lead you to conspire
That fatal evil deed,
I would then not have sought
One single glance or one sweet smile.
And with this letter,
The Baroness has thought,
How to unmask herself
To no more defile
The chastity of your wife Nina . . .
My time is precious: read it quickly.

(Arbenin looks at the letter and reads it)

Stranger: *(Raising his eyes upward, hypocritically)*
Oh, Providence, you'll execute the villain!
The innocent has perished. I regret!
But what awaited her was desperation,
And in its stead,
In Heaven she'll find her true salvation!
Ah, I took a glance at her: her EYES,
They mirrored clearly the chastity of heart.
Who would have thought this momentary flood
Would so harshly crush
This flower bud?
Why are you silent, wretch?
Tear
Your hair
And scream
"Oh, how horrible! How dreadful!"

Arbenin: *(rushing at them)*
Oh, I shall strangle you, my executioners!

(Suddenly he weakens and falls into his armchair)

Zvezdich: *(Shoving him roughly)*
             Repentance will not help you
             The problem hasn't been resolved.
             The pistols await here . . .
             He is silent.
             He does not seem to hear.
             Is that how he's lost his reason?

Stranger: Maybe.

Zvezdich: You've ruined it for me.

Stranger: Yes, our targets differ.
             Yes, I have just avenged.
             And you may find
             Your fair revenge.

Arbenin: *(rising and looking wild)*
             What have you said?
             I've lost my strength.
             But I was so hurt and so certain!
             Oh, God, forgive me, please . . .
             (He laughs)
             Send me your pardon.
             And those prayers, tears, and pleas . . .
             Did you forgive?
             (He kneels before the two men)
             Here I am, before you, on my knees.
             Oh, tell me, please,
             That her unfaithfulness and her deception
             Were so apparent!
             I beg and order you to state your accusation . . .
             Right now! Was she innocent?
             And were you here?
             But did you look into my heart?
             The way I'm imploring you

She was beseeching me so hard.
It's a mistake. How wrong I was!
I did not hear.
She told me
           That,
When she was going to die,
But I told her it was a lie!
(He rises)
Yes, I told her THAT . . .
(Pause)
And here's what I shall disclose to you:
It wasn't I, not I who's murdered her.
(He looks at the Stranger fixedly)
'twas you, admit and speak. Be brave!
My dear,
At least, with me, please, be sincere!
Why did you push her to the grave?
I did love her. If I could foresee,
Even to Heaven,
I wouldn't give one of her tears . . .
But I condone you.
(He falls onto the Stranger's chest and weeps)

Stranger: *(Giving him a rough push)*
           Get hold of yourself, Arbenin.
           (To Prince Zvezdich)
           Let's take him out,
           He'll surely come to senses there . . .
           (He takes Arbenin by the hand)
           ARBENIN!

Arbenin: For an eternity
           We shall go apart . . . And nowhere . . .
           Fare thee well . . . Let's go, go . . .
           This way, this way . . .

(He rushes into the door behind which Nina's coffin is placed)

Zvezdich: Stop him! Stop him!

Stranger: This proud mind has broken today!

Arbenin: *(Returning, with a wild groan)*
Here, please, look!
Just look!
(He runs to mid-stage)
Didn't I tell you,
You were so cruel?

*(He falls to the floor and sits in a
half reclining position, with a fixed stare)*

(Prince Zvezdich and the Stranger stand over him)

Stranger: I've waited long for full revenge,
And finally I am avenged!

Zvezdich: This man is happy . . . He's insane . . .
But I, forever and in vain,
Shall seek my peace and honor!

End of Act 4

APPENDICES

Mikhail Y. Lermontov, "The Masquerade"

(a poetic drama in four acts)

English translation: Alfred E. Karpovich, Ph.D.

A. Scenario

ACT 1

Scene 1:   <u>The 19th century "Playing House"</u> ("casino" was not used) in St. Petersburg Russia. Prince Zvezdich has lost a game of cards. Sprich (pron: "Shprikh"), a money lender, offers help but gets rejected. Arbenin (pron. "Ar-ben'-nin"), a wealthy middle-aged man, comes to the rescue: he sits down to gamble instead of Zvezdich. He wins and gives the cash to Zvezdich. Very excited, both want to relax at the masquerade in the hub of the Russian "BEAU MONDE". Sprich, a scheming man, rushes to the masquerade after Arbenin. Kazarin (pron.: "Kazahrin"), an old friend of Arbenin's and a gambler, intends to draw Arbenin, now a married man, back into gambling and to benefit from it.

Scene 2:   <u>The Masquerade</u>. Masks, crowds, walking up and down, plus Arbenin and Zvezdich. Some dance (A. Khachaturian composed a sentimental waltz specifically for this drama). Arbenin feels bored. He becomes a moralist for his new and grateful young friend. Zvezdich eagerly seeks a love affair. A female mask converses with him. The flirting woman seems to know Zvezdich. He feels intrigued and asks her for some gift as a keepsake. The lady picks up a lost bracelet from the floor and gives it as her own to Zvezdich.

She never takes off her mask. Then she leaves. Zvezdich swears to find her, and he shares his new experience with Arbenin. Arbenin thinks he may have seen this bracelet before. A male mask harasses Arbenin, then disappears. Arbenin is angry.

Scene 3 Arbenin is back at home. While awaiting his belated young wife Nina, he pines for his far-off turbulent youth. Nina returns late. He is jealous, and reassuring him, she says she is ready to quit "Beau Monde" and to become "a country lady". His jealousy increases when he learns from his man servant that Nina has just returned from the masquerade. Arbenin notices one of her two bracelets missing. Caress is gone. His countenance changes to menacing looks. Nina who claims innocence is in tears.

ACT 2

Scene 1 In Baroness Strahl's (pron. "Shtrahl") **House.** Excited, after flirting with Prince Zvezdich at the masquerade the night before, the Baroness, a young widow, cannot read her book. This lady of the Beau Monde reflects on her feelings for Zvezdich. Nina Arbenin, a friend of hers, walks in. After her small talk with the Baroness, Prince Zvezdich also shows up. All of them went to the masquerade last night. Zvezdich talks with Nina privately after he spots a bracelet on Nina's hand. It looks exactly the same as his "keepsake". She was seeking a similar bracelet in every store to replace her lost one. A "weird" idea occurs to Zvezdich that the female mask was Nina. Now he assures Nina of his love which infuriates her. After Nina leaves, Zvezdich shares his suspicion with the Baroness, who is now in panic. Sprich also shows up. The Baroness uses him as a tool to spread the dirty gossip about the "new relationship" between Nina and Zvezdich. Sprich agrees to do it, hoping to return the money he once lent to her deceased husband.

Scene 2 In Arbenin's House. Arbenin reflects on his new sad revelations. A note has arrived for Nina from some "Princess". It appears to be a love letter from Zvezdich slightly "corrected" by Sprich. Now Arbenin has "proof" of his wife's infidelity. While Arbenin is away from his study room, Sprich and Kazarin come in. From Sprich Kazarin learns of the "affair" between Nina and Zvezdich. Kazarin is determined to return Arbenin to gambling as his pal and partner, and to disturb him in his peaceful family life. Sprich watches Arbenin from afar and then leaves for the Baroness's place. The frustrated Arbenin succumbs to Kazarin's tales of the past. He is now in Kazarin's hands. He is a gambler again.

Scene 3 In Prince Zvezdich's House. Ivan, a servant, who protects Zvezdich, his master, in his sound sleep, lies to Arbenin who has just arrived: "my master isn't at home". While Ivan is away, Arbenin sees Zvezdich in the bedroom and feels tempted to kill him in his sleep but hesitates: he becomes "a coward under the pressure of enlightenment". Instead, he writes a message for Zvezdich. In the doorway, he runs into the Baroness. It seems his wife's "affair" is well-known to the Baroness. The enraged Arbenin accuses her of "teaching" "sinless victims" infidelity. The Baroness is about to disclose the truth, but Arbenin would not listen. He leaves. Zvezdich wakes up. The Baroness, fearing for his life, discloses the truth. Zvezdich takes it lightly: in the worst scenario, he would routinely challenge Arbenin to a duel. When the Baroness leaves, he reads the note from Arbenin: an invitation to visit N. tonight and "to have a good time".

Scene 4 At N's Place. The host, Kazarin, and Arbenin sit down to play. Arbenin anticipates a revenge. The host wants "to fleece the Prince a bit". Zvezdich arrives and plays cards. While playing, Arbenin mocks Zvezdich with his "funny stories". Zvezdich begins to lose lots of money. Upon a slight pretext, Arbenin accuses Zvezdich of cheating, names him "a scoundrel" and throws cards in his face. Zvezdich challenges Arbenin to a duel but Arbenin declines the challenge. His plan is different: he has dishonored Zvezdich publicly, and the Beau Monde will throw Zvezdich out. Arbenin is satisfied.

ACT 3

Scene 1   The ballrooms in the Beau Monde. The rumor works: Prince Zvezdich, a coward, fails to challenge his accuser to a duel. Aristocrats turn away from him and from Nina. Yet, Zvezdich is here. He cautions Nina against a grave danger and returns the lost bracelet. He intends to go to the Caucasus in order to wash away his disgrace with his blood in the war. Nina does not take his warning seriously. Arbenin watches them from afar, with his rage rising. The guests gossip about Baroness Strahl who is rumored to have left St. Petersburg for the country life. Music is heard (waltz, polonaise, etc.): The guests, including Nina, dance in the next ballroom. Arbenin is tormented with jealousy: he still loves Nina but now he has every proof against her. He always keeps a poisonous powder in his pocket for "a rainy day". Nina must die. It is too stuffy in the ballroom. The guests and the hostess ask Nina to sing something for them. With a clear premonition of an evitable trouble Nina sings a sentimental romance and plays the piano. When Arbenin walks in, she forgets the last couplet. Then she rests on the couch and asks her husband for an ice cream. He promptly brings it in, having put some poison in it. The premonition of a disaster is in the air. A Stranger watches the scene of poisoning but does not intervene. Arbenin and Nina go home.

Scene 2   Arbenin's bedroom. Nina's maid notices that her mistress is unusually pale. Nina recollects all the events of the day, in particular, the beautiful new waltz she danced. When Arbenin comes in, the maid leaves. He locks the door. Nina feels worse and worse. They converse about their failing love and the value of life. He denies her a doctor. He prepares her for death. He admits that she is poisoned. She dies innocent. Arbenin is in tears.

ACT 4

Scene 1 Arbenin sits on a couch. He suffers, still in doubt: was Nina innocent? Kazarin shows up for a few moments. He suspects a murder. Other people (a doctor, relatives) come in, discussing apparel for the funeral. The doctor suspects Arbenin's mental disorder. The doctor runs into Zvezdich and the Stranger in the doorway. After the doctor leaves, they see Arbenin who is deep in thought. The Stranger speaks to him. The Stranger lost a fortune gambling with Arbenin years ago. The Stranger's mind is full of revenge. He feels he must destroy Arbenin. Once he followed him at the masquerade. He also witnessed Arbenin's preparation for his murder. This is the moment of revenge: "Arbenin, Nina's murderer was you". Now it is Prince Zvezdich's turn to avenge. He shows the Baroness's letter to Arbenin. In her letter, the Baroness discloses the truth. Arbenin is totally insane and completely destroyed. While the Stranger is satisfied, Zvezdich remains un-avenged: in his miserable state of mine, Arbenin cannot be challenged to a duel. The evil is punished with insanity. The real murderer is the Beau Monde that kills both Nina and Arbenin. The Beau Monde exaggerates an aristocratic sense of dignity, and the intrigue of the shallow human mentality kills love. The drama is over.

B. Synopsis

This poetic (rhymed/blank versed and rhythmic) drama takes place in the 19th Century Beau Monde of St. Petersburg, Russia. Arbenin (the protagonist), a middle-aged nobleman, an ex-gambler and an ex-playboy, is now happily married to Nina, a very young lady of the Beau Monde. Arbenin treats Nina as his property. Once Nina claims she lost one of her two bracelets at the masquerade. The jealous husband suspects infidelity. His suspicion is soon "proven", though Nina claims innocence. Arbenin is certain she gave the bracelet for a keepsake to her "lover", Prince Zvezdich. Arbenin, a loving villain, passes his verdict to dishonor the Prince and to put his wife to death. He poisons Nina in the ballroom and denies a duel to the Prince. Soon enough the whole intrigue is unveiled. It was a young widow, Baroness Strahl, who had given the bracelet lost by Nina at the masquerade to Prince Zvezdich for a keepsake. Nina and the Baroness were close friends. Now that the Baroness learns about the tragedy, she no longer cares about her own reputation in the Beau Monde. In a letter she reveals the truth to Arbenin: Nina dies innocent. Another person (Stranger) from Arbenin's past shows up to avenge Arbenin. The Beau Monde, with its culture of honor and aristocratic dignity, victimizes four people: Nina is dead, Arbenin is insane, Prince Zvezdich is disgraced for life, and the Baroness becomes a country lady having left the Beau Monde for good.

Notes for Theater Repertorial Companies:

Four female roles available and six males. Nina sings her little romance. Nina and the other (nonverbal) ladies dance a waltz (by A. Khachaturian composed for "The Masquerade"). Nina mentions this "new waltz" in her monologue. "The Masquerade" was filmed in Russia, 1941.

C. Acknowledgments

It is my pleasure to thank the following distinguished people for their help in the course of my work. Among them are Professor Anatoly Liberman, University of Minnesota, for his friendly collegiate advice; Mr. Ben-Gurion Matsas, Editor-In-Chief of "Image Magazine", for publishing several early excerpts from this translation; Yevgheniy A. Yevtushenko, the distinguished poet and Professor of Tulsa University, for his appreciation of Nina's monologues in my translation and for his criticism. Last but not least, I thank Mrs. Rosa Matsas for her technical assistance and interest in my work. It would be unpardonable not to mention Mr. Roger W. Phillips, with his pioneering translation of "The Masquerade", in prose, in the 1970s. Most of M. Lermontov's works were translated by Soviet translators and poets in Moscow, USSR. A solid volume of "Major Poetical Works" by M. Lermontov was published, in A. Lieberman's translation, in Minneapolis, 1983. The spirit of my own translation is, no doubt, impacted by many of the previous serious works. The most recent volume of M. Lermontov's "Selected Works" was published in 2008, XMO, Moscow, Russia. I also appreciate Professor T. Bird's interest in this translation (Queens College, CUNY).

I am pleasantly indebted to a group of experienced editors who helped me all the way to see this book published. These are Mr. Ben Hudson, Mr. Jeff D. Stevens, Ms. Diane Lee, Ms. Sarah Disbrow, Ms. Cherry Noel, Ms. Sheryll Gomez, Ms. Grace Allen, and Mr. Jeff Hecita.